LOVE AND MONEY

A FARCICAL COMEDY IN TWO ACTS

by
RAYMOND HOPKINS

HANBURY PLAYS

**Keeper's Lodge, Broughton Green
Droitwich, Worcestershire WR9 7EE**

BY THE SAME AUTHOR

LOVE BEGINS AT FIFTY
IT MUST BE LOVE
THE LOVE NEST

PERFORMING RIGHTS

LOVE & MONEY

The Feltons live in a small town in the Midlands. The action of the play takes place in the lounge of their semi-detached house. It is late summer – the present day.

ACT ONE

ACT TWO

THE SETTINGS

Derek and Pauline Felton have been married for twenty-seven years. Their only child, Amy, is a nineteen-year-old petite girl, whose main interests are boys and animal rights.

Life has been passing by fairly smoothly for the Felton's, that is until they return home one evening to find that their house has been burgled.

Derek, who has always had a materialistic outlook on life, decides that their new house insurance will yield a lucrative pay out. Pauline becomes increasingly unhappy about his subsequent course of actions. The ensuing friction is exacerbated when Amy's latest boyfriend turns out to be the thief.

Joyce Clements, their next door neighbour, has witnessed the robbery. She calls in daily to offer support, advice and unwelcome comments.

To add to the mayhem, The Reverend Peter Jones, who has unexpectedly called round to invite Derek to read a lesson at a televised service, falls hopelessly in love with the Scenes of Crime Officer investigating the robbery.

The hilarious confusion which follows has a surprising twist at the end. This means the Feltons' lives will never be the same.

CAST IN ORDER OF APPEARANCE

DEREK FELTON About forty-eight. Has a very materialistic outlook on life. Not always truthful. Will grab every opportunity that the world offers, plus some that it does not.

PAULINE FELTON About forty-five. Down to earth, honest and sincere. A complete opposite to Derek, but that seems to keep the marriage alive.

THE REV. PETER JONES About thirty-three. A very saintly Christian who has given his life to the church. He is shy and naive when it comes to girls. His romantic passions have never been switched on.

JOYCE CLEMENTS About fifty-two. Slightly overweight. Very mixed temperament. Lives alone, next door to Pauline and Derek. Not much money, therefore, finds life hard going. Will need to have a change of appearance during play.

AMY FELTON About nineteen. Good looking and petite. Has very definite views on life, especially on animal rights. Likes a boyfriend whom she can dominate.

P.C. BEN DRAPER About twenty-five. A likeable person, but also a bit gullible. Someone you can easily feel sorry for. Smart in appearance.

ELIZABETH ANDERSON About twenty-five. Slim, attractive and intelligent. She has had lots of men friends, but never found that special one.

TONY PECK About twenty. Comes from a poor background. Not very well educated. Lacks communication skills. His favourite word is all right, which he pronounces orl-wight. Only child, has been dominated by his mother.

NOTE: When Tony Peck is robbing the Feltons' house he must not be recognisable.

ACT I

Scene I

Five minutes before the play starts, the curtain rises revealing a dimly lit stage. Tony Peck enters from kitchen wearing a balaclava. He systematically robs the house, exiting several times to kitchen with items of value. The main stage lights come on.

(Pauline and Derek enter from hall and stare around the room)

DEREK   What the hell ...?
PAULINE   Oh, Derek, whatever's been going on in here?
DEREK   *(Getting* cross) While we've been round your mum's, listening to her rabbiting on about her bunions, some yobbo's broken in and nicked everything we own.
PAULINE   I thought things like this only happened to other people.

(Derek and Pauline walk around room in a daze)

DEREK   Don't you believe it. Crime's the only growth industry this country's got left.
PAULINE   *(Pauline starts crying)* This is just like a nightmare.
DEREK   *(Giving Pauline a hug)* Now come on, don't cry. *(Derek spots his matchstick model on the cupboard)* That's a bit of luck. *(Letting go of Pauline and walking over to the cupboard)* At least he hasn't taken my matchstick model of Concorde. *(Holding up matchstick model and examining it. – The model can be made of balsawood)*
PAULINE   *(Stopping crying – getting cross)* Our house has been ransacked and all you're worried about is a pile of dead matches?
DEREK   This took me five years to build. It's precise in every detail. *(Putting down model and walking around room)*
PAULINE   What sort of person does this?
DEREK   Lowlife scum who are too lazy to work for money. If I get my hands on the lout, I'll break every bone in his body.

5

PAULINE   You may get a chance. He's probably still upstairs.

DEREK   *(Walking to hall exit)* We'd better wait outside. *(Unconvincingly)* You've got to be careful using violence on these criminals. We're into the compensation culture nowadays.

PAULINE   I'll ring the police. *(Pauline dials number)* Hello ... I want the police ... Oh, hello, we've been burgled ... Mrs. Felton, 26 Bloxham Way ... Our phone number's 736478 ... Please hurry, we're not sure if the burglar's still here ... Oh, right, bye. *(Pauline replaces receiver)* We're not to touch anything. They're sending a Scenes of Crime Officer round, to look for forensic evidence.

DEREK   So, while this yobbo's flogging off all our possessions, we've got some time waster here, puffing talcum powder everywhere.

PAULINE   These SOCO people catch far more burglars with today's hi-tech methods. *(Pause)* I still think we should check around the house.

DEREK   *(Sitting on sofa)* Give me a shout if you find anyone.

PAULINE   *(Getting cross)* And there was me thinking I'd married Macho man.

DEREK   All right, I'll go. *(He picks up a poker and, unseen by Pauline, exits to the kitchen)*

(Door bell rings. Pauline walks to hall exit)

PAULINE   That was quick. They must have got a rapid response car in the area. *(She exits to hall – off)* Come in. *(Pauline and Rev. Jones enter from hall. Rev. Jones is wearing a scarf round his neck and is carrying a case)*
Where would you like to start? We've not touched a thing.

REV. JONES   I was wondering if your husband's free on Sunday.

PAULINE   *(Looking puzzled)* Pardon?

REV. JONES   I'm sorry, I didn't introduce myself. I'm your local vicar, *(pulling his scarf away to reveal his clerical collar then putting it back)* Reverend Peter Jones. *(Shaking Pauline's hand)* I was hoping your husband would read a lesson at our Family Service.

PAULINE   Actually you've caught us at an extremely bad time. You see we've just been...

REV. JONES   It won't take a minute. I just need to have a word with him and explain what I'd got in mind.

6

PAULINE   The thing is, we've not been to church since my brother's wedding and he got divorced fifteen years ago.

REV. JONES   I like to encourage new sheep into the fold. *(Pause)* Try to <u>catch</u> the lost souls. *(Stands his case on the sideboard)*

PAULINE   *(Impatiently)* Oh, right, just wait there a minute, I'll get my husband. *(Exits to hall)*

(Rev. Jones opens his case and fiddles about with the contents)

DEREK   *(Entering from the kitchen and putting down the poker)* You didn't waste any time. My wife tells me you're always finding new ways of <u>catching</u> people. *(Walking over to Rev. Jones)* I suppose you get to meet the dregs of society in your job.

REV. JONES   *(Closing the case and facing Derek)* Well, we're all sinners in the Creator's eyes. *(Reassuringly)* Still the Bible tells us his redemption is boundless.

DEREK   *(Aside)* That's all I need, some born-again copper.

REV. JONES   We should all strive to follow in the Lord's footsteps by forgiving those who've wronged us.

DEREK   It's all right if you're living up there. *(Looking up)* I mean, the angels are hardly going round nicking each other's harps, are they? *(Getting cross)* If it was up to me, I'd chop their thieving hands off.

REV. JONES   Oh dear, that's not quite the response I was hoping for. I'm not sure what to do now.

DEREK   Instead of babbling on about all this redemption rubbish I suggest you cover yourself in talcum powder and get your equipment out.

PAULINE   *(Entering from hall)* Oh there you are. I see you've met the vicar.

DEREK   *(Standing still and looking horrified)* <u>Vicar?</u> But, I thought you were the SOCO man.

REV. JONES   *(Putting his case on the floor)* I'm afraid you've lost me.

DEREK   Aren't you supposed to wear a dog collar? Or are you some undercover agent?

REV. JONES   *(Pulling his scarf back and showing his clerical collar)* I've got a sore throat.

PAULINE   Reverend Jones wants you to read the lesson at the Family Service.

REV. JONES   It's the last Sunday of this month.

DEREK *(Patronizingly)* There's no need to worry about my salvation, Vicar. I've been nationalized, immunized, baptized and circumcised. *(Picks up Rev. Jones' case and hands it to him)*

REV. JONES Actually I received spiritual guidance, and was led to your home.

PAULINE *(Aside – to Rev. Jones)* After a few gins at the Nag's Head, he's normally guided home by the spirit.

DEREK I'd love to help, *(unconvincingly)* but that's the very day we've arranged to take mother-in-law to the … Um… *(Searching for excuse)* Zoo.

REV. JONES Oh dear, that's left me in such a dilemma. All the church members desperately want to read. It's causing so much bickering and backbiting.

DEREK *(Looking bored)* Really?

REV. JONES I did explain to everyone. It was only after much prayer and meditation I realised the Lord was leading me to someone unconnected with the church.

DEREK *(Pushing Rev. Jones to hall exit)* Yes, well, we must press on. We're dealing with far more earthly matters at the moment. *(He almost pushes Rev. Jones through the hall exit)*

REV. JONES Don't forget to watch the service on television. We've been chosen to take part in a nationwide broadcast.

DEREK Have we? I mean, have you? *(Pulls Rev. Jones back into centre of the room)* On reflection I may just be able to make it.

REV. JONES *(Looking confused)* But what about mother-in-law?

DEREK The animals can see her another day.

REV. JONES Oh right. *(Pause)* I've chosen a passage you'll recognize immediately. It's Psalm 23.

DEREK *(Looking vague)* Ah yes, that does sound very familiar … Um … it's on the tip of my tongue…

REV. JONES We'll be using *The Good News Bible*. Is that the one you have in your home?

PAULINE We've not had a bible since …

DEREK It got stolen. Haven't you told the vicar we've been burgled?

REV. JONES So your home's been broken into? How very sad.

DEREK He's even stolen our bible. *(Looking sad)* I'll really miss our family devotional times.

PAULINE It's only just happened. We were checking to see if the burglar was still here.

REV. JONES *(Looking worried)* I'll just pop out to my car and get you a bible. *(Runs through hall exit with case)*

DEREK   You could have warned me he was a vicar. *(Flippantly)* When he files his report on me, bang goes my chances of seeing the pearly gates.

PAULINE   That serves you right. I've never heard so many lies. *(Pause)* We don't own a bible, and you're only reading the lesson so you can be on the telly.

DEREK   You're only jealous 'cause he didn't ask you. *(Rev. Jones enters from hall carrying a large bible)* I was joking about cutting a thief's hands off. I'm all for helping the wayward wanderer.

REV. JONES   Let's hope we don't bump into any. *(Looks around room uneasily. Hands Derek the large bible)* I really must be going. I'll be in touch soon.

PAULINE   I'll see you out, Vicar. *(Exits to hall with Rev. Jones)*

DEREK   *(Standing and looking upward, holding the bible. Thinking aloud)* I can see it now, the choir singing in the background, the congregation sitting in silence and the whole nation awaiting my entrance. *(Pauline enters from hall)* I'm going to be a celebrity. I've always said I'm full of charisma.

PAULINE   You're full of something, but it certainly isn't charisma. *(Door bell rings)* That'll be the police. *(Exits to hall – Off)* Oh, hello Joyce, come in. *(Pauline and Joyce enter. Joyce is carrying several sheets of A4 paper)* You'll never guess what's happened?

JOYCE   You've been burgled. *(Looking pleased)* I witnessed the whole incident from my kitchen window. He got in through your back door.

DEREK   Why ever didn't you ring the police?

JOYCE   My phone's not working.

DEREK   Mrs White across the road's got a phone.

JOYCE   I've not spoken to her since she accused my cat of peeing over her garden gnome's fishing tackle.

DEREK   So you just sat and watched the burglar ransack our home?

JOYCE   From start to finish. *(Pause)* I didn't even get a chance to make a cup of tea.

DEREK   You should have made a citizen's arrest.

JOYCE   Citizen's arrest? I nearly had a cardiac arrest.

PAULINE He seems to have taken everything of value.

JOYCE   I know. It took him ten journeys to get it all on his van.

DEREK   I just can't believe you'd stand by and watch the entire contents of our home disappearing out the door.

JOYCE   *(Patronizingly)* Haven't you ever heard of Neighbourhood Watch?

DEREK   But you're not supposed to just watch, you're supposed to ...

JOYCE   Keep 'em peeled, and if you can't help, jot down all useful information. *(Joyce gives Derek the sheets of A4 paper)* Here's a list of everything he took.

DEREK   I just don't know what to say. *(Sinks into a chair)*

JOYCE   There's no need to thank me, Derek. It's what any good neighbour would do.

DEREK   Still, at least, you'd recognise him. I suppose we must be thankful for small mercies.

JOYCE   Well, actually, he was wearing a balaclava. Although he did take it off to blow his nose. *(With trepidation)* When I saw that gaunt face, under the street light, it sent a shiver right down my spine.

DEREK   I suppose you didn't think to get the number of his van?

JOYCE   *(Looking pleased)* It's the first thing I did. *(Pause)* Here, I've made a note of it. *(Gets a small piece of paper from her pocket and gives it to Derek)*

DEREK   Now we're actually getting somewhere. *(Reading from piece of paper)* Two chipolatas, three faggots, and something for fungal toenail infection.

JOYCE   *(Grabbing piece of paper)* That's my shopping list, *(looking at piece of paper)* but I threw that away. *(Pause)* Oh dear, I've thrown the wrong piece of paper away. *(To Pauline)* This robbery's got me all of a dither.

PAULINE   What time did he break in?

JOYCE   About an hour ago.

DEREK   So you've done absolutely nothing for the last hour?

JOYCE   Yes, I drank half a bottle of sherry and made several visits to the loo. *(Pause)* I must have missed you come in.

DEREK   That's a first. *(Getting cross)* You spend all your time lurking about behind your curtains, peering through your binoculars, and on the one occasion it could have been useful, you did nothing.

JOYCE   How dare you. *(Getting cross)* Are you trying to tell me I'm nosey?

PAULINE   Just ignore him, Joyce. *(Glaring at Derek)* He's a bit on edge at the moment.

10

JOYCE   He's not the only one. I got really annoyed watching the thief. *(Pause)* He took so long to rob you, I missed one of my favourite TV soaps. *(Pause)* If there's anything you want to borrow, let me know.

PAULINE Actually, I wonder if we could have a pint of milk? I forgot to get some this morning, *(to Joyce)* and I need a cup of tea.

JOYCE   Only too pleased to help. Let's get it now.

PAULINE   *(Sarcastically – to Derek)* Will you be all right on your own for a minute?

DEREK   *(Indignantly)* Of course I will.

(Pauline and Joyce exit to hall. Derek looks around room. Amy enters from kitchen unseen by Derek)

AMY   *(With disbelief and shock)* Whatever's happened, Dad?

DEREK   *(Jumping with fright)* Oh, Amy, it's you. *(Getting his composure back)* We've had a break-in.

AMY   What a mess. *(Looking worried)* Where's Mum?

DEREK   Next door, getting some milk. Amazing isn't it, how a cup of tea calms any crisis. *(With horror)* Oh, my God, I've just realized we're not insured. *(Sinks into a chair)*

AMY   Please tell me you're joking.

DEREK   No; a couple of years ago I was having an economy drive. So I cancelled our home insurance.

AMY   Nice one, Dad.

DEREK   We'd been paying into that wretched policy for the last twenty-five years. *(Getting cross)* It wouldn't surprise me if these insurance companies are in league with the 'Burglars Federation'. "It's okay to rob 26 Bloxham Way, we haven't got to payout anymore."

(Pauline enters from hall carrying a bottle of milk)

AMY   *(Giving Pauline a hug)* Oh, Mum, are you all right?

PAULINE   I will be, when I've had a cup of tea.

DEREK   It'll take more than a cup of tea to sort out our present predicament.

AMY   Dad's just told me, we're not insured.

PAULINE   Yes, we are.

DEREK   No, if you remember, I cancelled the policy when we'd finished paying off the mortgage.

PAULINE   So it's fortunate I took out a new policy.

11

DEREK   You what?

PAULINE   An insurance man phoned and offered to give me a quote. He called round last Wednesday and signed me up.

DEREK   *(Kissing Pauline)* Thank you, my darling. You're wonderful. *(Pause)* Just as a point of interest, how much are we paying?

PAULINE   Fifty pounds a month. He advised me to go for their 'platinum' policy. *(Getting cross)* You're not criticising my decision, are you?

DEREK   Of course not. It's just that insurance men are like car salesmen. They're all compulsive liars.

PAULINE   In that case, you'd do very well in the job. Now if you've quite finished I suggest you go and get the policy. It's in the dressing table drawer.

DEREK   *(Meekly)* I'm on my way, darling. *(Exits to hall)*

PAULINE   Let's hope we don't get any more days like this.

AMY   And to think, my evening started off so well. *(Pause)* I was in my evening class at tech, and this boy came walking in. I couldn't take my eyes off him. Then I realised he was looking at me. *(Dreamily)* It was as though no one else existed.

PAULINE   So your eyes met across a crowded room? That sounds original.

AMY   Don't mock, I'm serious. *(Getting excited)* He's absolutely gorgeous, Mum.

PAULINE   You fall in love every day of the week. *(Pause)* You'd better check what's been stolen from your room, while I put the kettle on.

AMY   Okay. *(Exits to hall)*

(Pauline exits to kitchen. Derek enters from hall, reading the insurance policy. He sits on the sofa. Pauline enters from kitchen)

DEREK   This policy certainly looks more upmarket than our old one.

PAULINE   The insurance man said the payments cost more, but you're buying peace of mind in this crime-ridden culture. *(Pause)* They pay the full new price of everything stolen. *(Getting form from cupboard draw)* He's left us this form to list down all valuable possessions.

DEREK   It's a bit late for that now. *(Looking thoughtful)* So they've no idea what expensive items we own?

12

PAULINE   No, he wanted me to fill out the form there and then, but I said I'd better check with you first. *(Pause)* I put it in the drawer and forgot all about it.

DEREK   *(Looking pleased)* That's a bit of luck. *(Pause)* I mean, that must put them in quite a dilemma.

PAULINE   *(Looking vague)* I suppose they'll have to rely on our honesty. *(Pause)* Still, once that forensic man finds some fingerprints, they'll soon catch the thief, and return our things.

DEREK   *(Using his jacket sleeve, he starts to dust everything)* What a pity the burglar didn't leave any.

PAULINE   *(Looking horrified)* Whatever do you think you're doing? We've been told not to touch anything.

DEREK   Look, I've spent my entire life flogging my guts out trying to make ends meet. This is the first opportunity I've ever had of getting some easy money.

PAULINE   I've never done anything dishonest in my life, and I'm not about to start now.

DEREK   This isn't being dishonest. We're the innocent victims in today's corrupt society. *(Finds a duster and continues to dust around the room)*

PAULINE   Will you stop that? *(Pause)* All right, I agree life's been a struggle, but we've got by.

DEREK   You can't look a gift horse in the mouth. Sometimes you've got to make things happen. This could change our lives forever.

PAULINE   You're right, you could end up in jail. *(Derek continues to dust around the room)* So are you saying you don't want the police to get our things back?

DEREK   No I don't. I'd say we're in line for a big payout, with this insurance policy. *(Pause)* It's like my dad used to say "If you turn your problems into prospects, you'll be a prosperous person."

PAULINE   That sounds like one of your dad's pearls of wisdom. *(Door bell rings. Pauline exits to hall)*

P.C. DRAPER   *(Off)* Good evening madam, P.C. Draper. I've called about the burglary.

(Derek stops dusting and hides duster under sofa cushion)

PAULINE   *(Off)* Oh, right. Come in. *(Enters with P.C. Draper)*

P.C. DRAPER   Evening. *(Pause)* Right, so approximately what time were you broken into? *(Gets out a notebook and starts to write)*

13

DEREK   About an hour ago.

P.C. DRAPER   Were there any witnesses to the robbery?

PAULINE)   Yes.

DEREK   )   No. Our neighbour saw the burglar, but he was wearing a balaclava.

P.C. DRAPER   *(Seriously)* Why would your neighbour be wearing a balaclava?

DEREK   No, the burglar was wearing the balaclava, *(aside)* you blockhead.

P.C. DRAPER   Oh, right.

DEREK   *(Looking at P.C. Draper)* You seem very young to be a police officer. Have you been in the force long?

P.C. DRAPER   I completed my training last month. I used to work in a burger bar, but realised I wasn't being stretched to my full potential. I'll just have a check round for the point of entry.

DEREK   He broke in the back door.

P.C. DRAPER   Won't be a sec. *(Exits to kitchen)*

DEREK   This is wonderful. *(Pause)* Things couldn't have worked out better.

PAULINE   Are you joking? That young officer's far too inexperienced. We'll never get our things back.

DEREK   *(Looking happy)* Do you know, I think you could be right.

PAULINE   In case you've forgotten, most of our possessions had sentimental value.

DEREK   So what? They had very little cash value. *(Pause)* I've always wanted a forty-two inch LCD television, with Dolby surround sound. We'll be able to afford a holiday in the Caribbean. I'll be watching scantily clad girls frolicking in the sea.

PAULINE   In your dreams.

P.C. DRAPER   *(Entering from kitchen)* He's certainly made a mess of your back door. You'll need to try and secure it tonight. *(Looking around the room)* Although there doesn't seem much point. *(Pause)* Right, is there any more information you can give me about the robbery?

DEREK   Not really. *(Looking hopeful)* I suppose we'll be filed away amongst the unsolvable crime statistics.

P.C. DRAPER   Don't worry, our Scenes of Crime Officer'll soon come up with some forensic evidence. We stand a good chance of returning your property.

DEREK   Most of the items were priceless. I expect they'll all be shipped abroad to some foreign collector.

PAULINE   *(Glaring at Derek)* I just can't believe I'm hearing all this.

P.C. DRAPER *(Sympathetically)* That'll be due to the shock of the robbery. The reality's sometimes difficult to face up to.

AMY *(Entering from the hall and starting to cry)* He's taken all the jewellery that Great Gran left me.

DEREK Don't worry, we'll list everything down on the insurance claims form.

AMY *(Amy cries)* He's stolen my photo album. *(Sobbing)* He's ransacked my room. *(Sobbing)* I just want Great Gran's jewellery back. It's all I've got to remember her by. *(To P.C. Draper)* You've got to help me.

P.C. DRAPER I'll devote all my time to catching this thief.

AMY Will you? *(Amy stops crying and hugs P.C. Draper)* Oh thank you so much. *(Makes eye contact with P.C. Draper)*

DEREK *(Aside)* Oh no, that's all I need. Some copper on heat.

AMY *(Kissing P.C. Draper)* I'd be eternally in your debt.

P.C. DRAPER *(Getting embarrassed)* I'll track him down night and day until I've recovered all your property.

AMY Do you really think you'll be able to? I'd reward you in whatever way I can. *(Amy kisses P.C. Draper again)*

DEREK *(To Amy)* Why don't you and your mum go and tidy the bedrooms? *(Aside)* Before this bobby bursts a blood vessel.

AMY *(To P.C. Draper – smiling)* See you later.

(Pauline and Amy exit to hall. P.C. Draper gets his composure back)

DEREK My daughter doesn't really want you to get her things back.

P.C. DRAPER But she's just begged me to do everything I can to find them.

DEREK You've got a lot to learn about women. Their brains are wired up differently to ours. They say one thing but mean another. *(Pause)* You see, my daughter's ex-boyfriend's let her down badly.

P.C. DRAPER I don't understand. *(Pause)* What's that got to do with me solving the crime?

DEREK All the stolen photos are of him. If she gets them back, all those painful memories'll return. It could send her into deep depression, again.

P.C. DRAPER So what did her boyfriend do that was so dreadful?

DEREK   He ran off with his yoga instructor. *(Pause)* One minute they were relaxing in the lotus position. The next it was full-steam ahead in the missionary position.

P.C. DRAPER   What a foolish man he is, leaving a lovely girl like your daughter.

DEREK   *(Looking thoughtful)* I've just come up with the perfect answer. Instead of looking for this elusive thief, you could help my daughter through these troubled times.

P.C. DRAPER   But I'm an officer of the law, not a prospective partner from a dating agency.

DEREK   There's a lot more to police work than fighting crime. My daughter's happiness is far more important than a few possessions. *(Pause)* She's certainly taken a shine to you.

P.C. DRAPER   *(Looking smug)* Do you really think she likes me?

DEREK   *(Unconvincingly)* It was absolutely obvious to me. *(Pause)* Look, I suggest you scale down the search, and concentrate more on my daughter's state of mind. You're just the tonic she needs.

P.C. DRAPER   What a responsible father you are, caring more for your daughter's welfare than the loss of all your personal possessions.

DEREK   Well, we are fully insured.

P.C. DRAPER   *(Walking to hall exit)* I'll go and have a chat to her now. Start the therapy as it were.

DEREK   No, wait 'til tomorrow. I mean, it'll give me chance to have a word with her first.

P.C. DRAPER   Oh, all right. *(Pause)* I'm certainly going to enjoy this side of police work.

DEREK   You'll be like a knight in shining armour, helping the damsel in distress. *(Pause)* This'll be our secret.

P.C. DRAPER   You can rely on me, discretion's my middle name. I'll be in touch tomorrow. Bye. *(Exits to hall)*

(Derek picks up Bible and insurance policy and studies them. Pauline enters from hall)

DEREK   Do you know, this is turning out to be the best day of my life?

PAULINE   Are you joking?

DEREK   Think about it. We've got a thief who's taken all our old junk, an insurance policy that'll pay out maximum premium, a policeman who couldn't find his own shadow, plus a vicar who thinks I'm the chosen one.

PAULINE   You've got it all worked out, haven't you?

DEREK   Too true. *(Looking upward)* So there is a God after all.

PAULINE   You're nothing but a hypocritical atheist.

DEREK   Thank you, dear. I'll take that as a compliment. *(Pause)* I'm going to be rich and famous. *(Holding up the Bible, and the insurance policy, and kissing them both)* Or as the Bible says, "GOD HELPS THOSE WHO HELP THEMSELVES." *(Pause)* I think it's time for that cup of tea.

Scene II

As the curtain rises, Derek is asleep in a chair. He has the Bible and insurance policy on his lap. He is snoring loudly. The door bell rings. Derek continues to sleep.

PAULINE   *(Entering from the kitchen)* The door bell's ringing. *(She walks over to Derek, hits him around the head, then exits to hall)*

DEREK   Ouch ...

PAULINE   *(Off)* Hello, Joyce, come in.

JOYCE   *(Entering from the hall with Pauline)* Hello, Derek.

PAULINE   Ignore sleeping beauty.

DEREK   *(Pretending to be asleep)* Ugh ...

JOYCE   Have the police caught anyone yet?

PAULINE   No, an officer called yesterday, but we're still waiting for the Scenes of Crime people.

JOYCE   Don't worry, once they've arrested the thief, I'll identify him. My memory's photogenic.

DEREK   *(Waking up – aside)* That's more than can be said for your face.

JOYCE   Were you insured?

DEREK   *(Putting Bible and insurance policy on the arm of chair)* Yes, but money's no compensation when all your life's treasures have been taken.

JOYCE   *(To Derek)* It's fortunate you didn't have any really valuable items. *(Awkwardly)* I mean, like antiques or expensive jewellery.

DEREK   *(Getting cross)* That's rich coming from you. Everything you own came from Sid's second-hand store.

17

JOYCE   That's not fair. *(Crying)* Since Frank walked out on me, it's not been easy.

PAULINE   *(Putting her arms around Joyce)* I know, Joyce, don't upset yourself. *(To Derek)* You've got a nerve.

JOYCE   *(Reflectively)* I gave that man the best years of my life, and all he gave me was a load of unpaid bills.

PAULINE   You want to forget about him, and find yourself a new partner.

JOYCE   *(Still crying)* I don't seem to be able to attract members of the opposite sex nowadays. Although I did go out with a farmer last week, but he only wanted me for one thing. And I'm sure you can guess what that was?

DEREK   *(Aside)* A scarecrow to frighten the pigeons off his crops?

JOYCE   It's not so easy to entice men when your body sags, and your face needs a daily helping of Polyfilla.

PAULINE   *(Enthusiastically)* I've got just the answer. You need a new image. Book a visit to the beauty salon. It'll work wonders for your ego. And who knows where it could lead.

JOYCE   *(Stops crying)* You could be right. *(Pause)* Perhaps I should lose a bit of weight?

DEREK   You could always have your jaw wired up. *(Aside)* That'd serve two useful purposes.

JOYCE   *(Sorrowfully)* I don't ask much from life. *(Pause)* Still, I mustn't burden you with my problems. I only popped round to get a progress report. *(With sadness)* I'll see you later. *(Exits to hall)*

PAULINE   How is it, every time Joyce walks through that door, you do your best to upset her?

DEREK   She rubs me up the wrong way. *(Pause)* My dad had a saying for neighbours like her. He'd say "She's <u>IN</u>considerate, <u>IN</u>quisitive, <u>IN</u>terfering and <u>IN</u> here far too often."

PAULINE   She happens to be my best friend and, since Frank left her, she's been very lonely.

DEREK   He only married her because he'd proposed when he was paralytic. *(Pause)* It put him off drink for life.

PAULINE   That man was a waste of space.

DEREK   She'd need a miracle, not a makeover to improve her looks. Her bathroom mirror should be getting danger money.

PAULINE   Now you listen to me. *(Getting cross)* You'd better start being exceptionally nice to Joyce, or I'm telling the vicar you're only reading the lesson to get on the telly.

DEREK   That's blackmail.

PAULINE   That's right. The minute you upset Joyce, I'm phoning the vicar. I'll soon put a stop to your fifteen minutes of fame.

DEREK   Okay, I've got the message.

PAULINE   I didn't sleep a wink last night. *(Pause)* I'll never feel comfortable living here now that man's been rummaging about in my drawers.

DEREK   *(Aside)* He should be so lucky. *(To Pauline)* You should look on the bright side. If we hadn't been burgled, we'd still be poor. *(Looking at his watch)* Talking of which, it's about time I rang the insurance people. *(Gets out of chair, picks up insurance policy and looks at it. He then dials number on the phone – speaking into phone)* Hello ... I wish to make a claim on my policy ... Mr Felton ... Oh right. *(Derek puts his hand over the phone)* They're putting me through to the claims department. *(Speaking into phone)* Hello ... I wish to make a very <u>large</u> claim. We've been burgled. <u>They've taken everything of value</u> ... Mr Felton, 26 Bloxham Way ... Yes, that's right ... We're platinum policy holders ... Oh, I see ... Bye. *(He replaces receiver)*

PAULINE   What did they say?

DEREK   They'll post us a claims form. Then a loss adjuster'll call. That's because we've not had a chance to list down valuable items. And within three weeks we'll be paid.

PAULINE   They certainly don't hang about.

DEREK   I'm going back to bed. You kept me awake all last night. *(Exits to hall)*

(The phone rings)

PAULINE   *(Answering the phone)* Hello ... Oh, hello, Joyce ... So you hadn't got your phone plugged in? Oh right ... What did the beauty salon say? ... Oh that's great ... So you're having the full works? ... I'll be round in about five minutes, and you can tell me all about it ... Bye. *(Replaces receiver)*

AMY   *(Entering from hall)* Hi.

PAULINE   Morning, dear.

AMY   What's happening about the burglary? Has that policeman got my things back yet?

PAULINE   Give him a chance. We've not even had the Scenes of Crime man yet. *(Pause)* Did you manage to get any sleep last night?

AMY   Yes thanks. *(Pause)* Tony woke me with an early morning phone call.

PAULINE   *(Looking puzzled)* Tony?

AMY   The boy I met yesterday. *(Looking dreamy)* Mum, I'm sure he's the one for me.

PAULINE   You haven't known the boy two minutes. *(Pause)* We know nothing about him.

AMY   It only takes one fleeting glance to discover your soul mate.

PAULINE   Just don't rush into anything. *(Pause)* What do you fancy for dinner tonight?

AMY   I'm not that hungry.

PAULINE   Your appetite'd soon improve if you packed in that stupid vegetarian diet.

AMY   *(Getting cross)* It's not stupid. We've no right to eat animals. It's barbaric.

PAULINE   People have always done it, ever since the first cave man tucked into a brontosaurus burger.

AMY   That's no justification. Animals have as much right to life as us. *(Pause)* You should be a vegetarian, Mum.

PAULINE   Whatever for? Animals haven't got any real brain power. They're just, well, they're …

AMY   Living creatures, with feelings, like us. *(With authority)* Don't you realise, we're distant cousins of the apes?

PAULINE   I can't believe that. *(Pause)* All the apes I've ever seen spend their days picking their nose and scratching their backsides.

AMY   Think about what you're saying. That's no different than your modern-day man, especially Dad.

PAULINE   Apes are only interested in seeing how much food they can stuff in their face.

AMY   No different than your modern-day man.

PAULINE   Apes are obsessed with sex.

AMY   )   No different than your modern-day man.

PAULINE)

AMY   I'll get you something from the supermarket. What do you fancy?

PAULINE   A couple of lamb chops, please.

AMY   You've not been listening to a word I've said. Just imagine those lambs, skipping about on a spring morning, not a care in the world. Little do they know that thanks to your carnivorous cravings, they're destined to be murdered, then slung on some supermarket shelf, between the tea bags and toilet rolls.

PAULINE   I couldn't eat them now. Not even with lashings of mint sauce and new potatoes.

AMY   That's your guilty conscience. *(Pause)* I'm bringing you a veggy surprise.

PAULINE   Oh all right. I'll give it a go.

AMY   Well done, Mum. You've just taken your first step in saving this planet from cannibalism.

(Amy exits to hall. Pauline sits on the sofa and reads the paper. After a few seconds the door bell rings. Pauline exits to hall)

P.C. DRAPER   *(Off)* Hello, I've called round as arranged.

PAULINE   *(Off)* Oh, right, come in. *(Enters from hall with P.C. Draper)*

P.C. DRAPER   Was that your daughter I saw driving off?

PAULINE   Yes, she's just popped out for a minute.

P.C. DRAPER   That was bad timing.

PAULINE   It's all right, you can tell me what's happening.

P.C. DRAPER   I think it's best if your daughter and I sort things out first.

PAULINE   In case you've forgotten, we've been burgled as well.

P.C. DRAPER   Ah yes, the burglary. *(Looking official)* I'm afraid there's nothing to report.

PAULINE   *(Impatiently)* So what are you doing here then?

P.C. DRAPER   Actually, it's a bit delicate. You see, I didn't pick up on the <u>vibes</u>. *(Pause)* It was your husband who put me in the picture.

PAULINE   Well, perhaps you'd be good enough to put *me* in the picture.

P.C. DRAPER   Oh dear. This is rather awkward. *(Looking smug)* Umm, let's just say your daughter's taken a fancy to someone she met yesterday.

PAULINE   I didn't realise my husband knew about that. *(Pause)* So what's that got to do with the robbery?

P.C. DRAPER   Well, nothing directly, but...

PAULINE   In any case I've told her, first impressions are often misleading. Although she insists she's found her soul mate this time.

P.C. DRAPER   Really?

(Derek enters from hall, unseen by P.C. Draper)

PAULINE   I assumed you'd be going straight to bed.

P.C. DRAPER   *(Looking shocked)* I beg your pardon?

21

DEREK   I couldn't sleep.

PAULINE   *(To Derek)* I'm slipping next door. *(Sarcastically to P.C. Draper)* If you actually make an arrest, perhaps you'd be good enough to let me know. *(Exits to hall)*

DEREK   I'm afraid you've had a wasted journey, I've not had a chance to speak to my daughter yet.

P.C. DRAPER   There's no need, she's already been pouring her heart out to your wife.

DEREK   *(Looking puzzled)* But my wife doesn't know anything about it.

P.C. DRAPER   The way things are going, *(putting his arm on Derek's shoulder)* I could soon be calling you Dad. *(Pause)* The only trouble is I'm away on a course for three weeks.

DEREK   *(Removing P.C. Draper's arm)* Now that is good news. After all, they do say absence makes the heart grow fonder. *(Pause)* I'll tell my daughter you'll be in touch soon.

P.C. DRAPER   Life's a funny old thing, isn't it? Nobody knows where Cupid's going to fire his arrows next. *(Pause)* See you soon. *(Exits to hall)*

DEREK   *(Aside)* Not if I see you first. *(Telephone rings. Picking up receiver)* Hello ... Who? ... Oh, right. Victim Support ... How kind ... Yes I'm fine thanks ... You don't pay out any money do you? No, we'll be fine ... Yes, I will, thanks for ringing. *(Replacing receiver. The door bell rings)* Oh no, what's 'Robo cop' forgotten now? *(Exits to hall)*

ELIZABETH   *(Off)* Good morning, Mr Felton? I'm Elizabeth Anderson, Scenes of Crime, my identification.

DEREK   *(Off)* Oh, right, you'd better come in. *(Derek and Elizabeth enter from hall. Elizabeth is carrying a large case)* Actually, I was expecting a man.

ELIZABETH   *(Aside)* That's probably what your wife said on her wedding night. *(To Derek)* You haven't touched anything, have you?

DEREK   No, my wife wanted to clean up, but I told her not to disturb the evidence.

ELIZABETH   *(Looking around)* I think I'll start in here. *(Removes a magnifying glass from her case and starts to look around room. Derek follows her very closely)*
Ah ... ha ... This looks promising. *(Examines a print on the sideboard. She goes to her case and gets her aluminium powder and brush)*

DEREK   It hardly seems worth wasting your time. You could be topping up the police pension fund by booking some unsuspecting motorists.

ELIZABETH   Look, I'm here to investigate a crime. So if you don't mind, I'd like to get on. *(Examines the print)* Now we're getting somewhere.

DEREK   *(Peering over Elizabeth's shoulder)* Are we?

ELIZABETH   If you're going to persist in following me around, perhaps you'd make yourself useful by hanging onto the dusting powder, and magnifying glass, while I get a lifting tab?

(Elizabeth goes to hand Derek magnifying glass and dusting powder. Derek drops them both behind the sofa)

DEREK   Whoops, butterfingers.

ELIZABETH   *(Bending down behind sofa and picking up magnifying glass)* You've broken the magnifying glass, and you've got dusting powder everywhere.

DEREK   Don't worry, I'll get a dustpan and brush. *(Exits to kitchen)*

(Elizabeth examines the broken magnifying glass. Derek enters from kitchen with dustpan and brush)

(Starting to clean up) I'll soon clean it up.

ELIZABETH   *(Getting cross)* No, leave it to me. You'll destroy all the evidence.

DEREK   That would be a shame. *(Stands dustpan and brush on sofa)*

ELIZABETH   *(Looking at magnifying glass)* We'd better see if we can stick this magnifying glass together. *(Pause)* You wouldn't have any glue, I suppose?

DEREK   We've got some superglue.

ELIZABETH   That should do it. *(Pause)* Let's give it a go.

(Derek gets some superglue from cupboard. The door bell rings. He stands superglue on sideboard)

DEREK   Excuse me. *(Exits to hall. Elizabeth stands magnifying glass on sideboard. She picks up dust pan and brush and disappears behind the sofa to sweep up dusting powder)*
(Off) Hello Vicar, come in.

(Rev. Jones and Derek enter from hall. They cannot see Elizabeth)

REV. JONES   There's a rehearsal tomorrow night at six.

DEREK   I'll be there. I think you're going to be very impressed with my performance.

REV. JONES   I've brought the passes to get your wife and daughter into the service. *(Hands Derek two tickets)*

DEREK   Is this really necessary? I mean the churches are always empty nowadays.

REV. JONES   There won't be a spare seat in the place.

DEREK   Sad, isn't it? What people'll do to get on the telly.

ELIZABETH   *(Appearing from behind the sofa)* Could we please get on? There's lots of people waiting for my services. *(Puts down dustpan and brush. Picks up superglue and magnifying glass from sideboard)*

REV. JONES   Goodness me, whatever's going on here?

DEREK   This is Elizabeth Anderson, our Scenes of Crime Officer. The Reverend Jones, a close family friend.

REV. JONES   *(Looking at Elizabeth with interest)* Pleased to meet you.

ELIZABETH   Could we please glue my magnifying glass back together, *(examines magnifying glass)* so I can finish examining this crime scene?

DEREK   I'm afraid I've accidentally broken this dear lady's equipment.

REV. JONES   Would you like me to have a look? I've always been a "do it yourself man." *(Pause)* When you live alone you've no choice.

ELIZABETH   How kind of you. It's nice to meet a real gentleman. *(Handing over superglue and magnifying glass to Rev. Jones)*

DEREK   We mustn't waste the vicar's time. There's probably some babies that need christening, or old folks that are ready for burying.

REV. JONES   May I suggest you pop into the kitchen and make a tea whilst I attend to this young lady's needs?

DEREK   Oh, all right, but I still think you're wasting your time. *(Exits to kitchen)*

REV. JONES   *(Examining magnifying glass)* Right, we'll need to pop some adhesive on here. If you'd just hold the magnifying glass we'll have this sorted out in a jiffy. *(Staring at Elizabeth with a*

24

besotted gaze. He doesn't pay any attention to the superglue he is applying)

ELIZABETH   Please be careful, Vicar. *(Pause)* You're squirting it everywhere.

REV. JONES   Just relax. In church they call me Mr Fix-it.

ELIZABETH   Surely you don't need all that? *(Rev. Jones squirts superglue everywhere)* Now you've got some on my dress.

REV. JONES   Leave it to me. *(Rubs his fingers on Elizabeth's dress)*

ELIZABETH   What are you doing?

REV. JONES   Just removing the surplus glue from your dress. *(Pause)* Oh dear, it doesn't seem to be working.

ELIZABETH   Let's forget the whole thing. *(Pause)* Would you please take your hand off me?

REV. JONES   Now that could be a little difficult. *(Pause)* My hand appears to be attached to your dress. *(Tries to pull his hand off Elizabeth's dress)*

ELIZABETH   *(Shouting)* Please tell me you're joking?

REV. JONES   Don't panic. *(Reassuringly)* Everything's under control.

ELIZABETH   You could have fooled me.

REV. JONES   If you just let go of the magnifying glass, then we can ...

ELIZABETH   *(Trying to let go)* I can't, my hand's stuck.

REV. JONES   *(Very calmly)* In that case, may I suggest, with your free hand, you take hold of the tube of superglue.

ELIZABETH   *(Getting hold of superglue)* Now that hand's stuck as well. *(Getting cross)* I don't believe this.

(Elizabeth and Rev. Jones now each have one hand stuck on tube of superglue. The Rev. Jones has his other hand glued to Elizabeth's dress. Elizabeth's other hand is glued to the magnifying glass, which in turn has now become attached to the Rev. Jones' jacket)

REV. JONES   We seem to have got ourselves into a bit of a mess.

(Rev. Jones and Elizabeth struggle for a few seconds. They finish up in a very compromising position on the sofa. Pauline enters from hall unseen by the Rev. Jones or Elizabeth who are rolling about on the sofa. Pauline stares in disbelief.)

ELIZABETH   So what do you suggest we do now?
REV. JONES   I'm not sure. We've worked our way through most of my ideas.

(Pauline looks horrified)

ELIZABETH   Perhaps we should try a different position. That might help.
REV. JONES   I'm willing to have a go at anything.

(Pauline coughs to get their attention)

ELIZABETH   Oh, hello.
PAULINE   I've not had the pleasure of meeting your wife, Reverend Jones.

(Rev. Jones and Elizabeth look very embarrassed)

REV. JONES   *(Indignantly)* This young lady's not my wife.
PAULINE   I'm sorry, how presumptuous of me. I just assumed that you and your girl friend were married.
REV. JONES   Actually, she's your Scenes of Crime Officer. *(To Elizabeth)* I'm sorry, I've forgotten your name.
ELIZABETH   *(Getting cross)* It's Elizabeth Anderson.
PAULINE   You certainly don't hang about, Vicar. You've not even bothered to learn the dear girl's name before rolling all over my sofa like Action Man on his wedding night.
REV. JONES   You've got it all wrong. We're stuck together.
ELIZABETH   *(Getting very cross)* The vicar's superglued us together whilst attempting to repair my magnifying glass.
PAULINE   *(Aside)* And there was me thinking you were trying to defrock each other.
DEREK   *(Entering from kitchen carrying three teas on a tray)* Tea up. *(Looking amazed)* Reverend Jones, what are you doing to our SOCO lady?
PAULINE   They've glued themselves together.

(Derek stands tray of tea on sideboard)

ELIZABETH   Look, would someone please just get me free?
PAULINE   *(Looking thoughtful)* Warm water's the answer. You've got to soak the glue in warm water.

REV. JONES   Yes, I've heard of that. The trouble is the glue's gone everywhere.

ELIZABETH   If anybody here thinks I'm relaxing in a Radox bath with the Reverend, they're mistaken.

PAULINE   *(To Derek)* Perhaps if you pull one side and I pull the other, we might just separate them.

REV. JONES   You could be right. I'd say the glue's not had the chance to form a bond yet.

DEREK   It's certainly worth a try.

REV. JONES   Right, let's go for it.

(Derek and Pauline help the Rev. Jones and Elizabeth off the sofa. Pauline gets behind Rev. Jones and Derek gets behind Elizabeth)

I'll give the command. On the count of three. *(Pause)* Ready, one, two, three. Everybody pull ...

ELIZABETH   Ahh ...

DEREK   And again, pull ...

REV. JONES   Keep going, there seems to be some movement.

(Some of Elizabeth's dress, – which could be held on with Velcro, rips off. The Rev. Jones and Elizabeth are still stuck together)

ELIZABETH   Ahh ...

REV. JONES   Whoops, that's torn it.

ELIZABETH   Don't just stand there gawking, do something.

REV. JONES   I feel a sermon coming on.

PAULINE   I'd say this is a job for the hospital.

REV. JONES   *(Staring at Elizabeth's body)* You don't think we should have one last pull, do you?

ELIZABETH   Certainly not. What do you think I am, a Christmas cracker? *(Pause)* Would someone please sort this mess out quickly?

REV. JONES   *(Staring at Elizabeth's body)* Don't rush on my account. I've no pressing engagements.

ELIZABETH   *(Getting cross)* Just get me to the hospital, *(pause)* now.

DEREK   It looks as though we've exhausted all other possibilities. *(Pause)* Come on, Vicar. I'll drive.

(Rev. Jones and Elizabeth exit to hall followed by Derek. Pauline tidies around the room. After a few seconds, Amy enters from hall carrying a vegetable pie)

AMY   *(Looking confused)* I've just seen Dad, getting into a car with a vicar embracing a half naked woman.

PAULINE   The vicar accidentally superglued himself to the SOCO woman whilst trying to repair her magnifying glass. Her dress got ripped off during our efforts to pull them apart. *(Pause)* They've gone to hospital to be separated.

AMY   Were there any injuries?

PAULINE   Only to the vicar's eyeballs as they leapt out of their sockets.

AMY   Here's your veggy pie. *(Amy hands over vegetable pie)* Tony's on his way round. We bumped into each other at the supermarket.

PAULINE   He seems to have a habit of popping up wherever you go.

AMY   He's everything I've ever dreamed of. He's good looking, kind, gentle, strong and so thoughtful.

PAULINE   He's also unique. *(Pause)* No other man living has all those qualities.

(Door bell rings)

AMY   That'll be Tony. *(Exits to hall. Off, in a dreamy voice)* Come in. *(Enters, followed by Tony who is wearing a hand knitted multi-coloured pullover, which is too large. He is holding a carrier bag)*
Mum, this is Tony.

(Pauline goes to shake Tony's hand, but he seems more interested in looking around the room)

TONY   All right?
PAULINE   Pleased to meet you.
AMY   Tony can't stop very long.

(Tony walks around the room, looking at the mess)

PAULINE   Oh dear, that's a pity. *(To Tony)* Have you got to get to work?

AMY   Tony's never worked. *(Pause)* He's frightened of making the wrong career move.

PAULINE   *(To Tony)* So what do you do all day, Tony?

TONY   *(Turning to face Pauline)* My mum's not been well, so I'm looking after her. I found this carrier bag on your doorstep.

AMY   What's in it? *(Takes carrier bag and opens it. She pulls out a photo album. Looking inside the album)* It's my photo album, *(rummages about in the carrier bag and pulls out some jewellery)* and all the jewellery that Great Gran left me.

PAULINE   Whatever's going on? *(Pause)* Why did the thief bring it back?

AMY   *(Giving Tony a hug)* This is wonderful, I've met Tony and now I've got all my things back.

PAULINE   Your dad's going to be in for a big surprise. He thought his life was destined for major changes.

AMY   Well he can stop worrying now. Everything'll soon be back to normal. *(Pause)* We probably won't even have to bother the insurance people.

TONY   *(Looking pleased)* So it's good news all round.

PAULINE   *(To Amy)* I'm not sure your dad'll see it like that.

AMY   I should think he'll be over the moon.

PAULINE   No, he'll probably be over the 'Nags Head' getting paralytic. *(Picking up telephone receiver)* I'd better ring the Samaritans. They'll need to be on stand by. Your dad's going to need intensive counselling to get him through this.

Scene III

As the curtain rises, Pauline is sitting on the sofa reading a newspaper. Derek enters from kitchen and exits to hall. After a few seconds he re-enters from hall.

DEREK   The tooth fairies haven't made another delivery then?

PAULINE   *(Looking up from newspaper)* What are you on about?

DEREK   Nothing else has mysteriously appeared on our doorstep.

PAULINE   It's early days yet.

DEREK   At this rate, I'll be an old age pensioner before we get all our stuff back.

PAULINE   The thief must be wrestling with his conscience or he wouldn't have returned Amy's things.

DEREK   *(Sarcastically)* So I suppose if he has a sleepless night, we could be watching our telly again? *(Pause)* Look, we've wasted enough time. I'm phoning the insurance people to get things moving.

PAULINE   Are you happy putting in a fraudulent claim?

DEREK   *(Getting cross)* There's nothing fraudulent about it. We've been burgled and now it's payout time.

PAULINE   You've not even informed them we've had some of our property back.

DEREK   I don't think the return of a few glass beads and some holiday snaps'll cause any major problems.

PAULINE   That's not the point. *(Gets off the sofa and walks to kitchen exit)* You know what I think. *(Exits to kitchen)*

DEREK   *(Picking up telephone and looking at the insurance policy, dials number. Speaking into phone)* Claims department please ... Mr Felton ... Hello, this is Mr Felton, 26 Bloxham Way. I'm enquiring about my household insurance claim ... Oh ... so the cheque's in the post? ... How much are we getting? One ... one ... one ... one ... hundred ... and ... fift ... fift ... fifty ... thousand ... one hundred and fifty thousand pounds ... tha ... thank you very much. *(Replaces receiver)* One hundred and fifty thousand pounds. *(Puts his arms into the air, clenching his fist)* Yes, one hundred and fifty thousand pounds. *(The door bell rings. He exits to hall – Off)* Hello Joyce, how nice to see you.

(Derek enters from hall followed by Joyce. Her hair has been dyed pink. She is heavily made up, completely over the top)

I must say you're looking rather gorgeous. *(Giving Joyce a kiss and a pat on the bottom)* That visit to the beauty salon's certainly made a difference.

JOYCE   Why have you been so nice to me over the last three weeks? *(Looking concerned)* Have you been stimulating your brain with an illicit substance?

DEREK   Of course not. I've just realised the world's not such a bad place, after all.

JOYCE   *(Aside)* It must be the mid-life crisis. *(To Derek)* Is Pauline in?

DEREK   I'll give her a shout. *(Walking over to the kitchen exit and shouting)* That adorable girl from next door's here.

(Pauline enters from kitchen)

I was just saying how lucky we are to have Joyce as our neighbour.

PAULINE *(Aside – to Derek)* All right don't overdo it. You've made your point.

JOYCE I've just had the gasman round to fix my cooker! I couldn't get rid of him.

DEREK He probably fancies you. *(Aside)* They enjoy servicing old boilers.

PAULINE Did you ring the insurance people?

DEREK Yes, they've put the cheque in the post.

PAULINE That's quick. How much are we getting?

DEREK *(Looking guilty)* Umm ... The girl on the phone didn't have all the details.

JOYCE I'm very pleased for you both. *(Getting envious)* It must be nice having a little windfall.

DEREK And don't think we're going to forget you, Joyce. You've been a wonderful friend to us over the years. *(Pause)* I've not said anything to Pauline, but I feel we should share our good fortune with you.

JOYCE *(Looking happy)* Oh ... well ... How kind ... Are you sure you want to start giving all your money away?

DEREK *(Taking a picture off the wall)* I want you to have this picture. We'll be adorning our house with some contemporary works, now.

PAULINE My gran gave us that.

DEREK Yes, I know, and I'm sure she'd want it to go to a good home. *(Hands Joyce the picture)*

JOYCE *(Looking disappointed)* Oh ... right, and there was me thinking I'd be getting a few readies.

DEREK I'm popping over to the off-licence. I think a celebration's in order. Champagne all right for everyone?

JOYCE I've never been one to refuse a drop of bubbly.

DEREK Will one bottle be enough?

JOYCE Well I don't normally drink much, at this time of day.

DEREK No, of course you don't. *(Aside)* I'd better make that two. *(To Pauline)* Oh, by the way, have you seen that bible the vicar left me?

PAULINE It's under that pile of *Sunday Sports* you keep for bedtime reading.

31

DEREK   Oh God, I slung that lot in the bin last night. *(Walking to hall exit)* I'd better go and rescue the bible.
JOYCE   You're too late. The dustbin men called this morning.
DEREK   I don't believe it. *(Pause)* I suppose I'd better buy the vicar another one. After all he is turning me into a superstar. *(Exits to hall, singing)*
(Off) "Oh what a beautiful morning."
JOYCE   I'd keep an eye on your husband. *(Pause)* Since my makeover, men have been swarming round me like bees round a honey pot.
PAULINE   So, what's that got to do with Derek?
JOYCE   He's been buzzing around me lately, giving me lustful looks.
PAULINE   He lost his appetite years ago.
JOYCE   Well, you can rest assured, I'll soon clip his wings if he tries anything. *(Pause)* Has the vicar recovered from his little accident?
PAULINE   He did have a glazed look about him when he called yesterday.
JOYCE   How embarrassing, being glued to that SOCO woman. Have you heard from her since?
PAULINE   She collected her case, last week, but now she's left a pair of gloves here. *(Pause)* If we're having drinks, I'd better put out a few nibbles.
JOYCE   I'll just pop home and lock my door.

(Pauline exits to kitchen. Joyce looks at the picture in disgust, then exits to hall. Pauline enters from kitchen carrying some crisps and nuts. Derek enters from hall)

DEREK   In all the excitement I forgot my wallet. *(Picks up wallet from table and looks for Joyce)* Has our nosy neighbour gone?
PAULINE   What, the one you fancy? *(Pause)* Joyce thinks you've got the hots for her.
DEREK   You're not seriously suggesting I'm attracted to that warthog, are you?
PAULINE   Well, you've certainly been laying it on a bit thick lately.
DEREK   I can't win, can I? I'm just being nice to her, as instructed by you. *(Pause)* Anyway, getting back to far more important matters. The insurance company are paying us

(shouting) ONE HUNDRED AND FIFTY THOUSAND POUNDS. *(Pause)* They've already posted the cheque to us.

PAULINE   Why ever would they pay us all that?

DEREK   I obviously convinced that loss adjuster to award us maximum dividend.

PAULINE   You didn't convince him. You conned him, after sending me out to the shops.

DEREK   Everybody exaggerates on their insurance claim. It's like fiddling your tax form. It's all part of the citizen's unwritten charter. *(Giving Pauline a hug)* We're just about to start enjoying the good life.

PAULINE   *(Pushing Derek away)* You've got it all worked out, haven't you?

DEREK   Too true. *(Pause)* That money's going to be a little nest egg for our future. *(Walking to hall exit)* I'll get that champagne. We've got some serious celebrating to do. *(Exits to hall)*

(Pauline makes herself busy. Amy and Tony enter from kitchen. Tony is wearing his multi-coloured hand-knitted pullover)

PAULINE   Hello, dear. Hello, Tony. *(Tony looks shameful and doesn't answer)*

AMY   You'd better go straight up to my room.

(Tony exits to hall. Pauline looks bewildered)

Oh, Mum, my whole world's falling apart. *(Amy cries uncontrollably)* Tony and I have had a dreadful row.

PAULINE   What about?

AMY   *(Amy stops crying)* I think you'd better sit down.

PAULINE   *(Sitting down)* This sounds serious.

AMY   *(Very quietly)* Tony's the one who removed the contents of our home, without our permission.

PAULINE   *(Standing up and shouting)* Are you telling me that your current boyfriend, the one you love beyond question, the one who's the answer to all your prayers, is the same person that ransacked our home?

AMY   Well, yes, I suppose you could put it like that.

PAULINE   I'll kill him. *(Walking to hall exit)* I'll kill him.

AMY   Hang on a minute, Mum, there is a simple explanation.

PAULINE   *(Turning to face Amy. Getting cross)* All our wordly goods have been stolen. I'm now a registered insomniac. Your

33

father's committed perjury and a virgin vicar's tasted the fruits of nature. *(Pause)* I'd like to hear your simple explanation.

AMY   Tony's mother wanted to go to Disneyland but they couldn't afford it. So Tony decided to fund the trip by robbing us.

PAULINE   *(Sarcastically)* Thank goodness she didn't fancy a world cruise, or he'd have needed a furniture van to rob every house in the street.

AMY   It's just that they were desperate for the money. *(Pause)* He realises now, he should never have done it.

PAULINE   Oh, well, I suppose it's something that he's showing remorse. *(Pause)* So he admits to his mistakes?

AMY   Yes, he said it was a mistake all right. *(Pause)* Even the junk shops didn't want our stuff. Everything's in his garage, it's getting in the way. He wants to bring it all back.

PAULINE   This just gets better by the minute.

AMY   I don't want Tony getting into trouble.

PAULINE   What seems absolutely incredible is that, after robbing us, he met you.

AMY   Actually, you're going to see the funny side of this. *(Pause)* You see, while he was robbing us, he found my photo and college pass and decided to chat me up.

PAULINE   So after taking all our property, just for good measures, he takes our daughter as well. I'll say one thing for him. He's got a bloody nerve.

AMY   Don't be angry, Mum, after all none of us is perfect. *(Pause)* I'll go and tell Tony you've forgiven him. *(Exits to hall)*

DEREK   *(Entering from kitchen carrying four bottles of champagne)* This is going to be a day to remember. *(Opening champagne)* Do you want a large drink or do you want an extremely large drink?

PAULINE   I suggest you pour out two extremely large ones.

DEREK   Good thinking. *(Derek pours out two large glasses of champagne)* As my dad used to say "When you've so much cash that you need a calculator to count it, you can't complain." *(Hands Pauline her drink)* Cheers!

PAULINE   What do you think of Amy's new boyfriend?

DEREK   Well, he's not the sharpest tool in the box. Still I suppose he's harmless enough.

PAULINE   Actually he's not quite as harmless as he appears. *(Pause)* He's the person who stole all our property.

DEREK   YOU WHAT? *(Pause)* The flaming little toerag. How ever could Amy get mixed up with a no-good yobbo like that?

PAULINE   He saw her photo when he was robbing us, and took a fancy to her.

DEREK   *(Slumping into a chair)* I can't believe this is happening to me.

PAULINE   So what are we going to do?

DEREK   I don't know about you, but I'm going to get stoned out of my mind. *(Puts his glass down and drinks from the bottle)* What a diabolical disaster.

PAULINE   It's the first time he's done anything like this. *(Pause)* His mum's not been well. He wanted to take her on holiday.

DEREK   Why couldn't we be robbed by a professional burglar? There should be a law against amateurs doing it.

PAULINE   He's got all our things in his garage. He wants to bring them back.

DEREK   This has got to be the worst news I've had since your mum said she was moving in just up the road. *(Taking several gulps of champagne from the bottle)* It was the one and only chance I've ever had to improve my life style. *(Taking several more gulps from bottle)* If only the stupid moron had left it just one more day before owning up! *(Taking several more gulps from bottle)* Hang on a minute. *(Getting excited)* We've already been paid. The cheque's in the post. We've got nothing to worry about.

PAULINE   I don't understand.

DEREK   *(Walking around the room)* It's simple. The insurance company's already given us the money. The minute they wrote the cheque they'd agreed on a settlement.

PAULINE   So what difference does that make?

DEREK   All the difference in the world. Tomorrow I'll bank the cheque and put it on special clearance. We've just got to stop that incompetent imbecile from confessing for the next twenty-four hours. After which time it doesn't matter, because the cash'll be in our account.

PAULINE   I don't like the sound of this.

DEREK   *(Convincingly)* Look, if I'd gone to the insurance company's office, the cheque would be in our bank by now. *(Pause)* It's all a question of timing.

PAULINE   Just how far are you prepared to go to get this money? You're already bordering on criminal activities.

DEREK   If that useless burglar had sorted out his retail outlets, none of this would be necessary. *(Door bell rings)* I'll go. *(Exits to hall – Off)* Hello Joyce, come in.

JOYCE   *(Entering from hall with Derek)* You haven't started without me, have you?

PAULINE   I'll put these crisps and nuts in a dish. *(Looking at Derek – Getting cross)* We've got to have a serious talk. I'm not happy about any of this. *(Exits to kitchen)*

JOYCE   Whatever's up with Pauline?

DEREK   *(Unconvincingly)* Umm ... Well ... *(Searching for excuse)* Since your transformation in that beauty salon, she thinks I'm paying you too much attention.

JOYCE   I knew it. *(Pause)* You must be careful, Derek, we're neighbours. *(Looking serious)* I'm Pauline's best friend.

DEREK   You're quite right. It's just that you're like a rare orchid that's suddenly come into full bloom. *(Gets bottle of champagne)* Let's have that drink. *(Pouring out drink)* Say when.

JOYCE   Keep going, keep going, keep going. That'll do nicely.

(Derek fills up two glasses and hands one to Joyce)

DEREK)
                        Cheers
JOYCE)

(They both drink. Amy enters from hall)

AMY   *(To Joyce)* Hi. *(Looking concerned – To Derek)* Tony's got to talk to you, Dad.

DEREK   Not now. Can't you see we've got a guest?

AMY   This won't wait. I'll go and get him, now. *(Exits to hall)*

JOYCE   Don't mind me, I'm looking forward to meeting Amy's new boyfriend.

DEREK   *(Derek spits drink everywhere)* I don't want him down here.

JOYCE   Derek this has got to stop. You're trying to get me on my own again. *(Pause)* I thought you said you'd got a grip of yourself.

PAULINE   *(Entering from kitchen. Handing out nuts and crisps)* Try a few nibbles, Joyce.

DEREK   Amy's bringing her boyfriend down to meet Joyce.

PAULINE   Of course, you haven't met him, yet.

DEREK   *(Aside to Pauline)* We can't let them meet. *(With desperation)* She'll recognise him as the thief. *(Pushes Pauline towards hall exit)* Just keep him upstairs, while I get rid of Joyce.

36

PAULINE I'm certainly not being party to your perjury. I'm bringing him down, so we can sort all this out, now.
DEREK No, don't, it'll ruin everything.

(Pauline exits to hall)

JOYCE This can't go on, Derek. Think of the consequences.
DEREK *(Looking thoughtful)* Actually, it's Amy's boyfriend I'm worried about. A lot of these young lads fantasize over the mature woman. *(Pause)* They dream about them being their sexual tutors.
JOYCE So what are you saying?
DEREK His hormones are rampant. His cravings for carnal knowledge'll go ballistic, once he sees the vision of desire you've become. *(Pause)* We must try and protect his innocence.
JOYCE I never realised what power I had over men. First you, Derek, now Amy's boyfriend. *(Looking thoughtful)* In any case, we're going to meet sometime.
DEREK Tomorrow'll be fine. *(Unconvincingly)* I mean, it'll give you chance to tone down a bit. Create a plainer image.
AMY *(Off)* Tony's coming to see you, Dad.
DEREK *(Grabbing Joyce)* Just nip into the kitchen. We don't want you unleashing a tidal wave of testosterone. *(Pause)* Perhaps you'd make a coffee while you're there. *(Pushes Joyce through kitchen exit just as Tony and Amy enter from hall)*
AMY Right, off you go, Tony.
DEREK *(Pretending to be busy, tidying up)* Not now, dear, can't you see I'm busy?
AMY You're not doing anything. In any case this won't wait. *(Looking at Tony)* Go on Tony, tell my dad everything.
TONY I'm very sorry, Mr Felton, but you see my mum's ... *(The door bell rings)*
DEREK Thank you God, saved by the bell! *(Exits to hall – Off)* Hello Vicar, you're an answer to prayer. *(Enters from hall with Rev. Jones)* I don't think you've met my daughter. This is Amy *(looking disgusted)* and her boyfriend, Tony.
REV. JONES Pleased to meet you. *(To Tony)* What an incredible jumper.
TONY My mum knitted it for me. She got the wool from old socks she'd unpicked.
REV. JONES So it's recycled? Very environmentally friendly.

TONY   It ponged a bit when I first put it on, but it's all right now.

AMY   Tony's mum spends all day knitting.

REV. JONES   Very industrious. *(Takes Derek to one side)* Have you seen your SOCO lady since our last meeting?

DEREK   She collected her things last week, but now she's left her gloves here.

(Tony and Amy continue in silent conversation)

REV. JONES   Such a perfect example of God's creation. *(Getting excited)* I wouldn't mind seeing a bit more of her.

DEREK   I think you saw quite a lot of her the other day.

REV. JONES   I meant she was very pleasant company. I became quite attached to her.

DEREK   Probably the superglue.

REV. JONES   *(Getting serious)* Have you ever fallen hopelessly in love?

DEREK   No, I got married instead.

REV. JONES   Until I met Elizabeth, I'd never realised what love was all about. *(Pause)* At college I dedicated all my time to study and, since then my life's been devoted to the Church.

DEREK   That's very commendable.

REV. JONES   Elizabeth's triggered off feelings I'd never realised existed. I can't sleep. I can't work. I can't concentrate on anything. I spend every waking moment thinking of her. *(Pause)* My brain's completely scrambled.

DEREK   That'll be due to the sudden exposure of a young firm female body.

REV. JONES   When God created man, I wonder if he realised the heartache he'd cause by creating woman? *(In a frantic manner)* The complex feelings of love, pain and mixed emotions are almost impossible to bear.

DEREK   You're reading too much into this. *(Pause)* Look, you're a red-blooded male. The simple fact is when God made us he gave half the human race curvaceous bodies, and the other half an overwhelming desire to play with them.

REV. JONES   Sorry?

DEREK   Think of the parable of the football player.

REV. JONES   *(Looking vague)* I'm not familiar with that one.

DEREK   The foolish player gets totally preoccupied with winning or losing. Whereas the wise player just enjoys the thrill of the game and the pleasure of scoring as often as he can.

REV. JONES   *(Looking vague)* You've lost me.

DEREK   It's playtime, Vicar. *(Pause)* You've just received a late call, from the bench.

REV. JONES   *(Looking shocked)* I think you're getting slightly confused between love and lust. *(Pause)* Still, I mustn't burden you with all my problems.

AMY   *(Walking over to Rev. Jones and Derek)* Have you got your sermon ready, Reverend Jones?

REV. JONES   I'm going to preach on the fraility of mankind. My text is, "Be sure thy sins will find thee out."

DEREK   Couldn't we have a sermon on the rich shall inherit the earth?

REV. JONES   Actually you've got that slightly wrong, in any case, I've received inspiration from on high.

AMY   That's it, the vicar's been given a message for you, Tony. *(To Tony)* Tell him what you've done. He'll soon sort things out.

TONY   I've got a confession to make.

(Tony goes to speak. Derek pulls Rev. Jones away)

DEREK   The vicar hasn't got time now. Don't forget he only works on Sundays.

REV. JONES   *(Preaching)* The troubled soul will never rest. The tortured mind has no place to hide. Make known the evil deeds that have festered...

DEREK   Don't give us a freebie sermon now. On Sunday you'll be able to get a collection.

REV. JONES   *(Turning to face Tony)* If there's something troubling you, my son, confess your transgressions, and the Lord will forgive you.

TONY   The thing is, Vicar, my mum's not been feeling very well, so I thought to myself, all right, let's book a holiday.

REV. JONES   What a caring soul you are.

PAULINE   *(Enters from hall)* Hello, Reverend Jones, how nice to see you.

DEREK   *(Pulling Pauline towards the Rev. Jones)* Get over here quickly.

PAULINE   What's the matter, now?

DEREK   (Aside – to Pauline) The vicar's brainwashing Amy's boyfriend. He'll soon be on his knees praying for forgiveness. We'll be singing "Alleluia, redemption is nigh" and I'll be kissing goodbye to all my lovely money.

PAULINE   When will you get it into your thick skull? That money's a fading pipe dream. You won't be getting it. You're living in cloud cuckoo land.

DEREK   I can't rely on you for anything, can I? In any case, Joyce has got a major crisis in the kitchen. She needs your help urgently. (Pushes Pauline through kitchen exit, then runs over to Amy and Tony, pulling them away from Rev. Jones) Amy, I want you and Tony to pop down to the shops urgently.

AMY   Not now, Dad, we're talking to the vicar. Tony's in a real dilemma.

DEREK   His dilemma'll have to wait. We desperately need some … Umm …

(Joyce pokes her head through kitchen exit. She does not spot Tony)

JOYCE   You're out of coffee. (Goes back into kitchen)

DEREK   That's just what I was going to say.

AMY   (To Derek) That's not urgent.

DEREK   (Taking Amy to one side) Of course it is. The vicar loves his caffeine. It's one of the very few pleasures he's allowed in life.

AMY   Oh all right, we'll go, but the minute we get back we're having a serious talk.

DEREK   If you say so.

(Door bell rings)

AMY   I'll get it. (Exits to hall)

ELIZABETH   (Off) I think I've left my gloves here.

AMY   (Off) Oh right, come in.

ELIZABETH   (Entering from hall with Amy) Did I leave my gloves here the other day?

DEREK   Yes, you did.

AMY   Let's get this coffee, Tony. (Exits to hall with Tony)

DEREK   I'll sort out your gloves. (Exits to hall)

ELIZABETH   I'm glad you're here, I owe you an apology. I was very rude to you the other day.

REV. JONES   Please don't apologise. I mean, after all, who'd want to be superglued to a vicar?

40

ELIZABETH   Actually, when it was all over, I saw the funny side of it. I've had quite a laugh. *(Elizabeth starts to smile)*
REV. JONES   It does you good to have a laugh.
ELIZABETH   I've got nothing to laugh about. *(Starting to cry)* My life's absolutely lousy at the moment. *(Crying loudly)* I hate my job. I can't afford the rent on my flat, and all the fur's dropping out of my hamster. *(Pause)* The vet hasn't got a clue what's causing it.
REV. JONES   Please don't cry. I'm sure your husband'll sort things out.
ELIZABETH   I'm not married. And the way things are going, I soon won't have anywhere to live.
REV. JONES   Now that really is good news.
ELIZABETH   *(Stops crying)* What do you mean?
REV. JONES   I think I've got the answer to all my prayers, I mean all your problems. You see I've a spare room in the vicarage which the diocese want me to rent out. It'll only be a nominal charge.
ELIZABETH   Do you mind having pets in the vicarage?
REV. JONES   Not at all. *(Pause)* You wouldn't be any good at secretarial duties I suppose?
ELIZABETH   Well, yes, I used to be a typist.
REV. JONES   I'm looking for someone to take on my office duties. The pay's negotiable and, if you take the job, the accommodation's free.
ELIZABETH   I can't believe things are working out so well.
REV. JONES   *(Aside)* Neither can I. *(To Elizabeth)* Why don't we pop over to the vicarage and I'll show you your room?
ELIZABETH   You're so kind and I don't even know your name.
REV. JONES   It's Peter.

(Pauline enters from kitchen)

ELIZABETH   I'm just popping over to Peter's bedroom. *(Exits to hall with Rev. Jones)*
PAULINE   There'll be a simple explanation.
DEREK   *(Entering from hall with gloves)* Where is everyone?
PAULINE   The vicar's just taken Elizabeth to his bedroom.
DEREK   My pep talk must have done him good. *(Pause)* So it's finally all coming together. The vicar's preoccupied in the bedroom. Joyce is busy in the kitchen. My cheque'll soon be in the

41

bank. All I've got to do now is send that bungling burglar home to his mummy, then everything'll be back on track.

(Tony and Amy enter from kitchen with a jar of coffee)

There's been a change of plan. The vicar's lost interest in his coffee. He's found something more fulfilling to whet his appetite. *(To Tony)* Your mum rang. She wants you to pop home because ... Um ... because ... Um ...

(Door bell rings)

I'll go *(Exits to hall)*
P.C. DRAPER   *(Off)* Hello, I'm back.

(Derek enters from hall, followed by P.C. Draper carrying a large bunch of flowers. P.C. Draper runs over to Amy and hands her the flowers)

Oh, my darling, I've thought of no one else but you. *(Kisses Amy passionately)*
TONY   Hey, what do you think you're doing?
P.C. DRAPER   *(Breaking off kiss for a moment)* Be a good chap and lock my bike up. *(Throws Tony a chain and padlock. He then goes into another passionate kiss)*
JOYCE   *(Entering from kitchen carrying a pot of tea)* I've made a pot of tea. *(Walking over to Tony)* Hang on a minute, I recognise you.

(Derek looks horrified)

~ Curtain ~

ACT II

Scene I

As the curtain rises, Pauline is sitting on the sofa and Amy is pacing up and down the room.

AMY   I've never been so embarrassed in my whole life.

PAULINE   I don't know what your dad's playing at. He'd told that policeman you fancied him.

AMY   It took me hours to reassure Tony I wasn't having an affair with some lusty law officer.

PAULINE   I still can't believe Joyce thought your boyfriend was her long lost nephew from Australia.

AMY   If only she'd recognised him, everything would have been sorted out by now.

PAULINE   Your dad didn't give her a chance. He soon got rid of everyone.

AMY   He's gone too far this time. *(Pause)* Where is he?

PAULINE   Banking the insurance cheque. At six o'clock this morning he was sitting on the front doormat waiting for the postman.

AMY   This isn't right, Dad's banking all that money while Tony's in a police station being grilled like some pork chop.

PAULINE   Well, it was his decision to give himself up.

AMY   You're treating Tony like some common criminal.

PAULINE   I hate to state the obvious, but he is a common criminal.

AMY   *(Getting cross)* When he's here, you never make him feel at home.

PAULINE   That is a bit difficult considering most of our home's in his garage.

DEREK   *(Entering from hall carrying a Bible)* Mission accomplished. *(Shouting)* We've now got one hundred and fifty thousand pounds in our account. *(Punching the air)* Yes.

43

AMY   Tell Dad that I'm not speaking to him. *(Folding her arms and looking into space)*

PAULINE   Your daughter's not speaking to you.

DEREK   Why ever not?

AMY   Tell him he's ruined my love life and given my boyfriend a criminal record.

DEREK   You can't blame me for your boyfriend's misdemeanours.

AMY   Tell him I most certainly do, and if anything untoward happens, he'll have Tony's blood on his hands.

DEREK   That's a bit melodramatic, isn't it?

AMY   I'm going to my room. *(Pause)* Perhaps you'd be good enough to let me know when Tony arrives. *(Exits to hall)*

PAULINE   You've made a real mess of things.

DEREK   Aren't you forgetting I'm the one who's just deposited one hundred and fifty grand in our account?

PAULINE   When are you going to realise your precious money won't buy happiness?

DEREK   No, I agree, but at least it allows us to be miserable in comfort.

PAULINE   You want to get your priorities sorted out. People are far more important than possessions.

DEREK   Look, I'm almost fifty. We've no aging relatives who are going to pop off and leave us a fortune. I think I've done rather well in securing our future prosperity.

PAULINE   Everything's money-orientated in your life. I sometimes wonder what's kept us together for the last twenty-seven years.

DEREK   You're making me sound terrible. I can't be all bad, I've just bought the vicar a new bible. *(Holds up a bible)*

PAULINE   That was only so you wouldn't ruin your chance of a television appearance. *(Pause)* However much did that cost? *(Pauline examines bible)*

DEREK   Thirty quid. It's identical.

(Door bell rings. Pauline puts bible on the sideboard and exits to hall)

PAULINE   *(Off)* Hello Tony, come in.

(Pauline and Tony enter from hall. Tony is wearing his multi-coloured pullover. He walks over to the sofa and collapses on it. Pauline exits to hall and shouts – off) Tony's here.

44

DEREK   *(Sarcastically)* That's right, make yourself at home.

(Pauline and Amy enter from hall. Amy runs over to Tony and starts stroking his forehead)

AMY   You poor thing, are you all right? *(To Pauline)* Mum, he needs a hot drink immediately. He's in a state of shock.

PAULINE   I'll make a cup of tea. *(Exits to kitchen)*

AMY   It's all over now, my darling. How did you get on?

TONY   All right, I told the police the truth, the whole truth, and nothing but the truth. *(Sorrowfully)* I poured out my entire life story.

DEREK   *(Sarcastically)* That must have had them riveted to their seats with excitement for at least two minutes.

AMY   *(Examining Tony)* Did they rough you up? *(Pause)* I wouldn't mind betting they'll slip in extra crimes to improve their clear-up rate.

TONY   Actually they were very nice. They gave me tea and fairy cakes. *(Pause)* I told them all about your insurance claim, Derek.

DEREK   You should have kept your mouth shut. It's got nothing to do with them.

TONY   They said they'd be in touch. Their enquiry's still ongoing.

DEREK   Well, they can close the files now. It's all signed, sealed and delivered.

AMY   *(To Tony)* I'm so proud of you, my darling. *(Kissing Tony)* You're my hero.

DEREK   Yes, well, I'd love to listen to your memoirs, but I'm dealing with far more urgent matters at the moment. *(Pause)* I'm getting a few more bottles of bubbly. I've got some serious celebrating to do.

AMY   I can't believe it. Tony could be scarred for life and you're boozing away over your ill-gotten gains.

DEREK   Well, if he doesn't want to join in, he could always go home, and help his mummy with her knitting. *(Exits to hall)*

AMY   *(Continuing to pamper and fuss Tony)* Are you sure you're comfortable, darling?

(Pauline enters from kitchen with a cup of tea)

TONY   Do you think I'll go to prison?

(Pauline gives Tony the tea)

AMY   Of course you won't. We'll appeal to the European Court of Human Rights, if necessary.

PAULINE   I think you're getting a bit carried away. They'll hardly hold an emergency summit over the plight of some petty thief.

AMY   My Tony's going to get the best defence that money can buy. *(Kissing Tony)* He's so stressed out at the moment.

TONY   Why don't we go to your bedroom? I could do with a lie down.

AMY   Good idea. It'll be more comfortable up there.

PAULINE   Hang on a minute, *(the phone rings)* Amy. I'd rather you stayed down here.

(Amy and Tony exit to hall. Pauline answers the phone)

Hello ... Yes ... I'm afraid he's out at the moment. Yes certainly ... So it's Mr Ross, the manager... As soon as he comes in ... Right ... Bye.

(Pauline replaces receiver. The door bell rings. Pauline exits to hall)

(Off) Oh hello, come in.

(Rev. Jones, Elizabeth and Pauline enter from hall)

REV. JONES   We've been busy furniture removing.

ELIZABETH   Peter's offered me a room, in the vicarage.

REV. JONES   Elizabeth's taking care of my secretarial duties. *(Pause)* Actually I was hoping to have a word with your husband about his reading.

PAULINE   I'm not sure where he is. I've just made a tea. I'll pour you both a cup while you're waiting. *(Exits to kitchen)*

ELIZABETH   Life really seems to be on the up for me now. I've found super accommodation, and a good job.

REV. JONES   I'm just pleased I was able to help. *(Awkwardly)* Perhaps we could go out for a meal sometime? *(Pause)* I mean, to cement our new working partnership.

ELIZABETH   Sounds good to me.

REV. JONES   *(Getting excited)* I'll book a table, the minute I get home.

ELIZABETH   The only thing is, you'll need to give me a bit of warning. You see *(getting excited)* I've met this new man.

REV. JONES *(Looking horrified)* What new man?

ELIZABETH   Last night, I decided to go out for a drink. Anyway, I was sitting watching the world go by, when this drop dead gorgeous bloke came up, and started chatting to me. We got on so well, it was as though we'd known each other for years. *(Pause)* Do you know, I've really got the feeling this could be the start of something special.

REV. JONES   *(Unconvincingly)*   Oh, I'm very pleased for you.

ELIZABETH   I've never been lucky in love, but this time I think things might just work out.

REV. JONES   Really?

ELIZABETH   Still, I mustn't bore you with my love life. *(Pause)* I suppose you're not into all that sort of carry on?

REV. JONES   Even vicars have feelings.

ELIZABETH   *(Awkwardly)*   I just meant … *(Pause)* I'll go and give Mrs Felton a hand with the tea. *(Exits to kitchen)*

(Rev. Jones sinks into a chair and stares into space. Derek enters from hall carrying three bottles of champagne. He tries to hide them when he sees the Rev. Jones)

DEREK   Oh hello, Vicar. I'll just pop this lemonade into the cabinet. *(Pushes the champagne bottles into the back of drinks cabinet)* Is everything okay?

REV. JONES   *(Sorrowfully)* Couldn't be better thanks.

DEREK   And how's your new lady friend?

REV. JONES   I've just been deluding myself. Elizabeth hasn't got any romantic feelings towards me. *(Pause)* When God made man, to some he gave wit, to some he gave wisdom, and to some he gave good looks. But to others, such as me, he gave less obvious gifts.

DEREK   Oh dear, that sounds very profound. *(Pause)* By the way, I've finished with your bible.

REV. JONES   Bible?

DEREK   *(Picks up bible from sideboard)* The one you loaned me for my reading.

REV. JONES   I took that back the other day. It was needed for the woman's meeting. *(Pause)* I'm sorry I should have told you.

DEREK   Oh, right. This must be ours. It's almost identical. *(Aside)* That's thirty quid down the drain.

REV. JONES   Still, at least you'll be able to resume your family devotional times.

DEREK   Oh, yes. *(Unconvincingly)* That'll be wonderful.

(Elizabeth and Pauline enter from kitchen carrying the tea and cakes)

PAULINE   *(To Derek)* Oh there you are.

(Pauline walks towards Derek. He thinks the cup of tea is for him. Pauline walks passed Derek and hands the tea and cake to Rev. Jones)

I've a nice piece of cake for you, Vicar.
REV. JONES   *(Sorrowfully)* I seem to have lost my appetite. Just a small piece, please. *(Takes the tea and cake)*
DEREK   *(To Pauline)* Did you make me a tea?
PAULINE   It's in the pot.
DEREK   Thanks a million.

(Elizabeth's mobile rings. She puts her cup of tea on sideboard and answers her phone)

ELIZABETH   Hello ... *(Sensuously)* Oh hello ... Yes I'd love to ... Hang on a tick... *(Puts her hand over the mouthpiece of phone – To Pauline)* Thanks for the tea, I'm so sorry but I've got to dash. See you all soon, bye. *(Removes her hand from mouthpiece and speaks into phone whilst heading for hall exit)* Where are you? ... Right ... I'm on my way... Oh, that's fantastic ... *(Exits to hall)*
REV. JONES   I really should be going. *(To Derek)* Don't forget we've got a final rehearsal tonight, at six-thirty. Bye.
DEREK   Oh, right. I'll see you later, Vicar.

(Rev. Jones puts his tea and cake on sideboard and exits to hall)

PAULINE   Whatever's up with the Reverend Jones? He's not touched his tea or cake.
DEREK   He fancies Elizabeth, but he's just discovered her affections lie elsewhere.
PAULINE   The poor man, and he's such a gentleman. Oh, that reminds me, a Mr Ross, the bank manager, wants you to ring him.
DEREK   Amazing, isn't it. I've used that bank for the last twenty years, and he's never even given me a glance, but the minute we've got some money he's all over me like a rash. Well,

he'll have to wait. I'm picking up my new suit for my television appearance. *(Exits to kitchen)*

(Pauline drinks her cup of tea. Tony and Amy enter from hall. Tony's hair is ruffled and he has his pullover on back to front)

AMY   Tony's more chilled-out now.

PAULINE   Is that why he's wearing his pullover back to front? *(Pause)* I'd better finish the ironing. *(Exits to kitchen)*

TONY   *(Looking pleased)* I've got a bit of good news. My mum rang the Job Centre, yesterday. She's got me a job. *(Changes his pullover the right way round)*

AMY   Oh Tony, that's wonderful.

TONY   I'm going to be working with animals.

AMY   *(Giving Tony a kiss)* Oh, my darling. I'm so proud of you.

TONY   They're giving me four years training and a frock, I mean smock.

AMY   It sounds very specialised. What sort of job is it? *(Pause)* Don't tell me you're helping out in the animal welfare sanctuary?

TONY   No, I'm going to be a butcher. *(Punching his fist into the air, with elation)* All right.

AMY   *(Getting cross)* This just isn't going to happen. I'd rather you return to a life of crime that earn blood money.

TONY   Don't worry, I'll be all right.

AMY   *(Shouting)* There's no way you're working in a butchers.

TONY   Why not? Like my mum says, "It's the job for me all right 'cause we'll be getting loads of cheap meat.".

AMY   *(With anger)* Well tell your mum that her precious son'll soon be living on a diet of rice and soya beans.

TONY   But I'm a meat and three veg man.

AMY   That's just too bad. I don't want to hear another word about it. *(With the same pronunciation as Tony)* All right?

TONY   All right. *(Pause)* I'd better let my mum know how I got on at the police station. She worries about me.

AMY   *(Getting cross)* When you're next in your garage I'd like to have my C.D. player back.

TONY   I've got it on the van. In fact I've got quite a few of your things on my van. *(Pause)* I'll bring them in.

AMY   I'll give you a hand. *(Exits to hall with Tony)*

(The phone rings. Pauline enters from kitchen and answers it)

PAULINE   Hello ... Oh hello, Joyce ... What's the weather like on the coast? ... So you're having a fantastic time on your weekend break ... You've decided to stay another day ... Right, we'll see you Tuesday ... Bye.

(Pauline replaces receiver and exits to kitchen. Amy and Tony enter from hall carrying a large cardboard box. They put it on the table and take things out of it. Tony removes a small television and stands it on the matchstick model of Concorde, smashing it to bits. Amy connects up the C.D. player and plays Paul McCartney singing 'Yesterday.' They put other items around the room)

AMY   It's starting to look like home again. *(Pause)* Fancy a dance?
TONY   Yea, all right.

(Tony and Amy start dancing. Derek enters from hall carrying his suit. He turns off C.D. player. Tony and Amy stop dancing)

DEREK   Whatever's going on in here?
AMY   Tony's decided to give us our property back.
DEREK   He can't give it back. It doesn't belong to us any more.
TONY   So what am I supposed to do with it, Derek?
DEREK   Don't tempt me, or I may just tell you.
TONY   I thought you'd be pleased.
DEREK   Shall I tell you how you could please me? Load all that stuff back onto your van right now, and then disappear into the sunset with it. *(Aside)* Preferably never to be seen again. *(Exits to hall carrying his suit)*
TONY   I think I should check on my legal rights. Could I use your phone?
AMY   Of course you can.
TONY   Have you got the insurance people's number?
AMY   *(Searching around)*   It's here somewhere. *(Finding insurance policy)* Ah, here it is. *(Hands Tony insurance policy)*
TONY   *(Looking at policy)* Thanks. *(Tony dials number)* Hello ... My name's Tony Peck, I robbed 26 Bloxham Way. They've made a claim. You've paid them, but now I've given them everything back... Yes ... The only problem is that Derek Felton's told me he doesn't want it back ... All right ... *(Looking at phone)* 736478 ... Bye. *(Replaces receiver)*

AMY   What did they say?

TONY   They're going to check with head office. The girl said she's never dealt with a situation like this before. She's going to ring me back.

DEREK   *(Derek enters from hall without his suit)* I thought I told you to load all that stuff back on your van. *(Looks at the television stood on his matchstick model of Concorde)*
I don't believe it. Some cretin's smashed my Concorde.

TONY   That was me. *(Pause)* Sorry, it was an accident.

DEREK   *(Examines matchstick model of Concorde)* Your whole life's one big accident. You're nothing but a doomsday disciple.

TONY   I have got some good news for you, Derek.

DEREK   What's that, you're emigrating?

TONY   No, I've rung the insurance people and sorted out our little problem.

AMY   Tony's informed them he's returned our property.

DEREK   *(To Tony)* Why are you doing this to me?

TONY   *(To Derek)* They're checking with head office to find out what happens now. The girl's phoning me back.

DEREK   *(To Amy)* However could you get involved with such a moron?

TONY   The girl on the phone wasn't a moron. She'd never dealt with anything like this before.

DEREK   *(Shouting – to Tony)* I was talking about you, not the insurance operative.

TONY   That's not very nice, Derek. *(Pause)* I bet you wouldn't say that if my mum was stood here.

DEREK   Stuff your mum. I know where I'd like to shove her knitting needles. Why have we been lumbered with her cast off?

TONY   *(To Amy)* I've got the feeling your dad don't like me.

DEREK   That's the understatement of the century.

(The phone rings)

TONY   *(Walking to phone)* It's all right, Derek. That'll be for me.

DEREK   *(Pushing Tony out of the way)* Get out of my way. *(Picks up phone)* Hello … Oh hello, Mr Ross, how nice to speak to the bank manager after all these years. So what did you actually want, to start playing stocks and shares with my money?… You what?… How could he?… An accident … If you say so … Bye. *(Replaces the receiver. He is in a state of shock)*
(To Tony) Have you got a brother who works at the bank?

51

TONY   No, my mum decided not to have any more children after giving birth to me.

AMY   Whatever's happened, Dad?

DEREK   My insurance cheque's been destroyed by some junior clerk on his first day at work. He spilled his coffee all over it. *(Pause)* The bank manager's told me to get the insurance company to issue another one.

TONY   I can't see them sending you another cheque, now that I've told them I've returned your property.

DEREK   This is a nightmare. *(Pause)* I'm going to wake up in a minute. *(Sits on chair with his head in hands)*

AMY   I've just thought of something. Now Tony's returned your things, and the insurance cheque's been destroyed, the police'll have to drop all charges against Tony. There's no case to answer.

TONY   Does that mean I won't be going to prison?

AMY   Of course you won't, my darling.

TONY   So you could say everything's turned out all right?

AMY   *(The door bell rings)* I'll go. *(Exits to hall – Off)* Oh hello, come in.

(Amy and P.C. Draper enter from hall)

P.C. DRAPER   Concerning our ongoing enquiries regarding the robbery. *(Looking happy)* I'm afraid I'll have to ask you to accompany me to the station. *(Walks towards Tony, but goes past him and puts his hand on Derek's shoulder)*

DEREK   Whatever for, I've done nothing?

P.C. DRAPER   Exactly, Sir. You were shielding the identity of a thief. Ever heard of perverting the course of justice?

DEREK   I'm sorry, but I can't possibly come. I've got the final rehearsal for my television appearance this evening.

P.C. DRAPER   Your television appearance'll have to wait, because my sergeant won't. He wants to have a friendly chat to you. *(Pause)* He said if you don't come of your own accord, I'm to arrest you. *(Looking happy)* I have been trained in the use of force, *(leads Derek to hall exit)* so I suggest you come quietly. *(Exits to hall with Derek)*

AMY   I'd better let Mum know what's going on, and I'd better ring the vicar. He's going to need a substitute reader for his lesson.

Scene II

As the curtain rises, Derek is sitting on the sofa staring into space. Amy is sitting on a chair, sobbing.

AMY   Tony's mum had no right to stop him seeing me.
DEREK   That stupid bank clerk had no right to spill coffee all over my insurance cheque.
AMY   *(Sounding indignant)* Why would his mum say I was insensitive to her boy's needs?
DEREK   I'd say you've had a lucky escape. In fact it's the one and only bit of good news I've heard recently.

(Pauline enters from kitchen)

My whole world's been shattered.
PAULINE   When are you two going to stop wallowing in self-pity, and get on with your lives?
AMY   How can I? Tony's never coming back. *(Pause)* No one understands what I'm going through. *(Stops crying)*
DEREK   Compared with me, you're having a ball. I've been deprived of my fifteen minutes of fame. I've wasted thirty quid on a Bible, my Concorde's been crushed, I've kissed goodbye to my jet-set lifestyle and now we've got all our old junk back.
PAULINE   Oh, that reminds me, the washing machine's playing up.
DEREK   Wonderful.
PAULINE   It's making a terrible noise, like a squawking crow. It keeps going, *(making the sound of a squawking crow)* ahrr... ahrr...
DEREK   That'll be the bearings.
PAULINE   Can you do it?
DEREK   Of course I can. *(Making the sound of a squawking crow)* Ahrr... ahrr...
PAULINE   No, you wally, I mean can you fix the washing machine?
DEREK   Oh, best you get the repair man in. *(Pause)* My life's falling apart at the moment.
PAULINE   You wait till you get some real problems to face, then you'll realise what life's all about.
DEREK   My dad had a saying for times like this ...

53

PAULINE *(Getting cross)* I'm not interested in your dad's saying. My gran had one saying that summed up life. She'd say, 'Yesterday's history. Tomorrow's a mystery. Today's a gift.'

DEREK *(To Pauline)* You can't tell me you're not upset over losing all that money.

PAULINE As long as we've got enough to pay the bills it doesn't matter.

DEREK All I wanted was to escape this mundane existence we call living. *(Pause)* Haven't you ever been envious of the freedom and security that the wealthy of this world enjoy?

PAULINE It's all relative. The more money you have, the more you want. It's like climbing a never-ending ladder.

DEREK All I'm asking is to be allowed off the bottom rung.

PAULINE What happens in life, happens. You're dealt the cards and you play with the hand you've been given.

AMY My pack's full of broken hearts.

DEREK My pack's been ruined by some joker.

PAULINE This is like living with a couple of manic depressives.

DEREK It was my one and only chance of improving my lifestyle.

PAULINE The only difference between a rich man and a poor man is that one sails his boat in the bath, and the other sails his boat on the sea.

AMY *(Crying loudly)* My Tony's sailed off into the sunset, without me. *(Stops crying)*

PAULINE For goodness sake, I can't take any more of this doom and gloom.

(The door bell rings)

That'll be the Jehovah's Witness, come to tell us that the end of the world is nigh. *(Exits to hall – Off)*
Oh hello, you'd better come in.

(Pauline and P.C. Draper enter from hall)

I hope you're the bearer of good news, or you could be investigating a couple of suicides.

P.C. DRAPER As it happens, I have brought some good news. *(To Derek)* All charges have been dropped against you, sir.

DEREK It's a bit late, now you've ruined my television debut.

AMY *(Getting cross)* You should have charged that little toerag, Tony. He needs locking up.

P.C. DRAPER   You're being a bit harsh on your boyfriend, aren't you?

AMY   You mean, ex-boyfriend.

P.C. DRAPER   *(Looking pleased)* Oh, now there's a turn-up for the books. *(Pause)* Well, I can't stop long. I'm meeting one of my dog-handling colleagues.

DEREK   What are you sorting out, some crime at Crufts?

P.C. DRAPER   Actually, I'm going to specialise in the Force by becoming a dog handler.

AMY   I didn't realise you liked animals.

P.C. DRAPER   Let's just say, *(looking at Derek)* they give you far less hassle than the human species.

AMY   Animals give unconditional love. *(Pause)* I'm a vegetarian.

P.C. DRAPER   I decided to be a vegetarian the day I finished at the burger bar. *(Pause)* I told myself, I'll never be party to animal abuse again.

DEREK   Yes, well, if you two are having an in-depth discussion on animal rights issues, I'm going to fix that broken shelf in your bedroom, Amy.

PAULINE   I'd better come and make sure you don't knock the wall down. *(Exits to hall with Derek)*

AMY   So what do you do when you're not fighting crime? *(Stands by P.C. Draper)*

P.C. DRAPER   I go out with my mates, for a drink.

AMY   What about your girlfriend, does she enjoy socialising?

P.C. DRAPER   I don't have a girlfriend, at the moment.

AMY   Really? *(Looking into P.C. Draper's eyes)* What made you kiss me the other day?

P.C. DRAPER   *(Getting embarrassed)* That was a genuine misunderstanding. I was under the impression you had feelings for me. *(Pause)* I must be getting on. Duty calls as they say.

AMY   Do you ever go to 'The Rooftop Club?'

P.C. DRAPER   Yes, I often pop in for a quick half.

AMY   Why don't you pop in on Saturday night? I'll be down there with my mates.

P.C. DRAPER   Oh right. *(Looking pleased)* So I'll see you Saturday?

AMY   I'll look forward to it.

P.C. DRAPER   *(Walking to hall exit)* Bye.

AMY   I'm popping over the road to the shops. I'll join you. *(Exits to hall with P.C. Draper. The phone rings)*

PAULINE *(Entering from hall and answering phone)* Hello ... Oh, hello, Joyce ... So you've just got back? ... Calm down, Joyce ... Right, so you've got lots of news, wonderful ... Yes, pop straight round ... I'll put the kettle on ... *(The door bell rings)* I must go, there's someone at the door ... See you soon. *(Replaces receiver and exits to hall – Off)* Hello Reverend Jones, come in.

(Pauline and Rev. Jones enter from hall)

REV. JONES I've just called to see how your husband is.
PAULINE I think I can safely say, he's had better weeks. I'll give him a shout. *(Pauline exits to hall – off)* The vicar's here to see you. *(Enters from hall)* Fancy a cuppa?
REV. JONES That sounds good to me.

(Pauline exits to kitchen. Derek enters from hall)

DEREK Hello, Reverend Jones. *(Pause)* I'm so sorry I wasn't able to make the service. I was unavoidably detained. *(Pause)* Complete misunderstanding of course.
REV. JONES *(Patronizingly)* Of course.
DEREK And there was me all ready to spread the good news of the gospel to the sinners of this world.
REV. JONES You could always read for us this Sunday.
DEREK Actually, I've just remembered, I'm a bit busy this Sunday. *(Pause)* Still, enough about me. How are things working out with your new house guest?
REV. JONES *(With sadness)* I'm thinking of asking Elizabeth to move out.
DEREK But the dear girl's only just moved in.
REV. JONES It's the last thing I want to do. But I just can't cope with the heartache. Each time I see Elizabeth it tears me apart. I never realised that love could inflict so much pain. *(Pause)* I stupidly thought she may have some feelings towards me. How wrong I was.
DEREK Of course, she's just met the man of her dreams.
REV. JONES Her dreams, my nightmare. *(Sorrowfully)* My job's to give strength, guidance and comfort to my parishioners. However can I do that, when my own life's engulfed with emotional turmoil? I've even contemplated ringing the bishop to see if I could be moved to another parish.

DEREK   Things will improve. *(Pause)* There isn't a man living who hasn't had his heart broken by some pretty girl. *(Pause)* Give it time.

REV. JONES   That's just it. Time's standing still for me at the moment. *(Pause)* The church organist told me he'd been though a similar situation. The trouble was he fell in love with a married woman in the choir.

DEREK   So did they make sweet music together?

REV. JONES   No, fortunately he resisted temptation by keeping himself busy. He raised lots of money for the church roof fund by getting people to sponsor him for playing his way through the hymn book. It took him days.

DEREK   And did it dampen his ardour?

REV. JONES   Yes, it kept him on the straight and narrow. *(With innocence)* Although he did say, the minute he starts playing the organ, all those lustful thoughts return.

DEREK   I'm sure they do.

REV. JONES   I've decided to give it a go. *(Pause)* Keep myself busy. I'm hoping it'll get me through these next few days.

DEREK   Talking of which, I must press on. I'm in the middle of fixing a shelf for my daughter.

REV. JONES   Can I help? It'll be very theraputic for me.

DEREK   Only too pleased. *(Exits to hall with Rev. Jones)*

(The door bell rings. Pauline enters from kitchen and exits to hall)

PAULINE   *(Off)* Oh hello, come in. *(Entering from hall with Elizabeth)*

ELIZABETH   I just called on the off chance that Peter was here, only I've left my key in the vicarage.

PAULINE   He was here a minute ago.

(A loud bang from upstairs)

REV. JONES   *(Shouting – Off)* Ahh ... That hurt.

PAULINE   He's obviously helping my husband fix a broken shelf. *(Pause)* How's the new man in your life?

ELIZABETH   A total disaster. *(Pause)* The rotten maggot forgot to mention he had a wife and four children.

PAULINE   Oh dear. Still, I'm sure Mr Right'll turn up one day. *(Pause)* Would you like a tea now you're here?

ELIZABETH   That'll be lovely. I'll give you a hand.

(Pauline and Elizabeth exit to kitchen. Amy enters from the hall. She goes over to the C.D player and selects a disc. She plays Leo Sayer singing 'Have you ever been in love?')

REV. JONES   *(Entering from the hall)* I've been sent down to see if you really need a shelf in your bedroom, only we're having slight problems fixing it.

AMY   Of course I need a shelf. Oh, I'll go and sort it out. My dad's useless. *(Amy exits to hall. Rev. Jones walks to hall exit. Elizabeth enters from kitchen)*

ELIZABETH   Just the man I want. *(Pause)* Do you take sugar in your tea?

REV. JONES   No, thank you.

(Elizabeth walks towards the kitchen exit. Rev. Jones follows her)

Actually. I was hoping to have a word with you, in private.

ELIZABETH   Won't be a sec. *(Pops her head through kitchen exit)* No sugar for Peter. *(Coming back into room)* Right, I'm all yours.

REV. JONES   Oh dear, this is very awkward. *(Pause)* I'm not sure how to put this.

ELIZABETH   It's me you're talking to, Peter. Come on, out with it.

REV. JONES   The thing is … Umm … The thing is …

ELIZABETH   *(Impatiently)* The thing is, what?

REV. JONES   , Well, you see … Umm … *(Unconvincingly)* I've got this friend. Who's got this problem.

ELIZABETH   *(Looking puzzled)* What sort of problem?

REV. JONES   There's this girl, who he thinks the world of. In fact he's deeply in love with her.

ELIZABETH   How romantic.

REV. JONES   No, it isn't, because she doesn't realise how he feels about her. *(Pause)* The trouble is, they live next door to each other. He sees her every day. It's almost unbearable for him.

ELIZABETH   Well that's simple. Tell your friend to ask her out. *(Pause)* Problem solved. Okay? *(Walks towards the kitchen exit)*

REV. JONES   No it's not simple at all. You see she's already got a boyfriend.

ELIZABETH   *(Turning to face Rev. Jones)* A boyfriend? *(Pause)* Oh dear, that does complicate matters slightly.

REV. JONES   My friend's thinking of moving away so he's not reminded of her daily.

ELIZABETH   That sounds a bit drastic.

REV. JONES   There doesn't seem any alternative. It's almost breaking my heart. I mean, my friend's heart.

ELIZABETH   Surely he could have a chat to her. Tell her how he feels. *(Pause)* Who knows where it could lead?

REV. JONES   The thing is, he's painfully shy.

ELIZABETH   Well, if he's hoping to start a relationship, he'll need to talk to her at some point.

REV. JONES   I realise that, but my friend finds it impossible to express his true feelings when he's with this girl.

ELIZABETH   That's certainly a difficult one.

REV. JONES   So it's best if they move away from each other? *(Pause)* Then my friend can get his life back together.

ELIZABETH   *(Looking thoughtful)* No he shouldn't give up that easily. *(Pause)* Hang on a minute. There's always the eye test.

REV. JONES   But there's nothing wrong with my friend's eyes.

ELIZABETH   No, silly. He's got to make eye contact with the girl.

REV. JONES   I don't understand?

ELIZABETH   Words aren't always necessary. If there's any chemistry between them, it can be triggered off by eye contact. Feelings of love and affection can just take over.

REV. JONES   So what are you saying?

ELIZABETH   Tell your friend the next time he meets this girl, have a quick chat, about anything, like the weather, what's on telly, or life in general.

REV. JONES   That sounds easy.

ELIZABETH   Then he's got to get as close to her as he can, without making her feel uncomfortable. *(Moves close to the Rev. Jones)*

REV. JONES   *(Fiddling about with his clerical collar)* Just like you're doing.

ELIZABETH   Exactly, now this is very important. *(Pause)* He's got to make eye contact. *(Looking into the Rev. Jones's eyes)*

REV. JONES   *(In an agitated state)* What good will that do?

ELIZABETH   If there were any sensual feelings between them. *(Sensuously)* That's when the chemistry would take over, and he'd find out if she had any feelings towards … *(Goes into passionate kiss with Rev. Jones)*

PAULINE *(Entering from the kitchen with tea)* Would anyone like some cake? *(Looking at Rev. Jones and Elizabeth)* I'll take that as a no.

(Rev. Jones and Elizabeth break off kiss)

REV. JONES *(In a dazed state)* I'm on my way to heaven.
ELIZABETH Don't leave just yet, we need to talk about this.
DEREK *(Off)* I need you up here, Reverend Jones.
REV. JONES *(Looking upward)* He's calling me. I've got to go. *(Runs through hall exit)*
ELIZABETH Wait a minute, Peter. *(Elizabeth sits on sofa and stares into space with a smile on her face.)*
PAULINE Are you all right?

(The door bell rings. Pauline stands tea on table and exits to hall. Elizabeth continues to sit in stunned silence.)

(Off) Hello, Joyce, come in.

(Joyce and Pauline enter from hall. Joyce is not so heavily made up. She looks good)

JOYCE I've got so much to tell you. *(Pause)* This weekend's changed my whole life. *(Spots Elizabeth)* Oh, hello.
PAULINE Of course, you two haven't met. *(Pause)* This is Elizabeth, and this is our neighbour, Joyce.
JOYCE Pleased to meet you.
ELIZABETH I need to have a word with Peter, urgently.
PAULINE Don't forget your tea.

(Elizabeth runs through hall exit)

JOYCE She's obviously got other things on her mind.
PAULINE So what's this fantastic news you've got to tell me?
JOYCE You'd better sit down. You're never going to believe what's happened to me.

(Rev. Jones enters from hall)

PAULINE This is our local vicar, Reverend Peter Jones.
JOYCE Hello, I'm Joyce from next door.

(Rev. Jones runs through kitchen exit)

Doesn't have much to say, does he?
ELIZABETH *(Entering from hall)* Peter, come back here. *(Exits to kitchen)*
JOYCE Whatever's going on?
PAULINE Don't ask me.
JOYCE Now, where was I? Ah, yes, I don't know whether I'd told you, but the guesthouse where I stayed was owned by one of my old schoolmates.
PAULINE I didn't realise that.
JOYCE I always had a crush on him as a teenager, but things never worked out.
REV. JONES *(Entering from kitchen)* I've just seen the promised land.
PAULINE I'm very pleased for you, Vicar.

(Rev. Jones runs through hall exit)

JOYCE It must be divine intervention.
ELIZABETH *(Entering from kitchen)* Peter, just hang on a minute. *(Runs through hall exit)*
PAULINE I'd say there's definitely been some earthly assistance.
JOYCE As I was saying, we'd lost contact over the last few years, but a mutual friend had told me about his guesthouse. So I decided to visit him. When I got there he told me that his wife had passed away.
PAULINE Oh dear, how sad.
JOYCE Anyway, we got chattering one night. *(Pause)* It was as though we were reliving our teenage years. After a few drinks, we realised we'd still got feelings for each other.
PAULINE This sounds interesting.
JOYCE *(Hesitantly)* The thing is, well ... the thing is ... Umm ... I've told him I'll move in with him. To help run the guesthouse. *(Pause)* You see he's finding it difficult on his own.
PAULINE You what? *(Pause)* You can't.
JOYCE Why not? I'm single, I've no commitments. And the way things are going, it could lead to a full-time relationship.
PAULINE But you can't move away. *(Pause)* We've been friends for years.

JOYCE *(Putting her arms around Pauline)* Don't you think I know that? *(Pause)* Sometimes you've just got to go with your instinct.

PAULINE But it's all so sudden.

JOYCE It's what I want. A new start. *(Pause)* He's already said he'll make me a partner in the business.

PAULINE Oh, Joyce, are you sure about this?

JOYCE I've never been so certain of anything in my life. *(Pause)* You can come and visit anytime. We'll never lose touch. The guesthouse overlooks a quaint harbour. It's beautiful.

AMY *(Entering from hall with Derek)* Hello, Joyce. Did you have a nice weekend break?

JOYCE It's been lovely, thanks.

DEREK The vicar's asked if we could leave him and Elizabeth alone for a few minutes.

AMY Perhaps he's going to surprise us by popping up the shelf in my bedroom.

DEREK *(Aside)* It wouldn't surprise me if something else was popping up in your bedroom.

JOYCE I don't want to upset you, Derek, but I'm afraid I've got some bad news.

DEREK After what I've been through this month, nothing you could say would upset me.

JOYCE Actually, I've got some very good news and some very bad news.

DEREK Let's start with the bad news, get it out of the way.

JOYCE I'm moving away, to live on the coast.

DEREK Oh. *(Pause)* I wanted to hear the bad news first.

AMY *(Getting cross)* Dad.

JOYCE You are a tease, Derek.

PAULINE I just can't get my head round this.

AMY *(Giving Joyce a hug)* Oh, Joyce, we're going to miss you so much.

DEREK So if that's the bad news. What's the good news?

JOYCE I feel very awkward saying this. *(Quietly)* You know that picture you very kindly gave me? *(Pause)* Well, I'm not really into pictures so I ...

DEREK Please don't tell me you want to bring it back?

JOYCE No, I decided to give it to my friend at the guesthouse where I stayed.

DEREK That's fine, by me. So that was the good news?

JOYCE   I've not quite finished yet. You see when I arrived at the guesthouse I noticed a small art gallery next door. So before giving my friend the picture, I decided to find out some details about it.

DEREK   *(Looking bored)* Oh, right, very interesting.

JOYCE   When I showed the picture to the owner of the art gallery, he just stared at it in stunned silence.

DEREK   Probably trying to think of something polite to say.

JOYCE   Actually, he begged me to sell it to him.

DEREK   Well, there's a turn-up for the books. So what did he offer?

JOYCE   Five hundred ...

PAULINE   Well done, that's brilliant.

JOYCE   So I decided not to give the picture to my friend after all. *(Pause)* I'm going to sell it. That's if it's all right with you?

PAULINE   Of course it is, at least one of us has had a bit of good luck.

DEREK   So is it back to the beauty salon to spend the five hundred quid? You might even get a bit of plastic surgery for that sort of money.

JOYCE   No, you don't understand. They've offered me *(shouting)* five hundred thousand pounds.

DEREK   YOU WHAT?

JOYCE   The picture you gave me is worth five hundred grand. Apparently it's an early work by some famous artist.

PAULINE   So you're saying it's some lost masterpiece?

JOYCE   Yes. *(Pause)* I'm going to be rich.

PAULINE   Well done, I'm so pleased for you, Joyce. *(Pauline gives Joyce a hug)*

JOYCE   The art gallery owner's had it authenticated. I've got all the documentation round home. I'll pop and get it. *(Joyce exits to hall)*

DEREK   *(Slumps into chair and cups his hands around his head)* This can't be happening to me. Has anyone got a gun?

PAULINE   I think it's great. Joyce deserves a bit of good luck.

DEREK   I don't mind her having some good luck, but not at my expense.

AMY   You're the one who gave her the picture, Dad.

DEREK   Thanks a million. That makes me feel a whole lot better.

PAULINE   Look, nothing's changed. What you've never had you don't miss.

AMY   Mum's right. What's done is done.

DEREK   So it's back to the drudgery of the daily rat race? The treadmill us human androids call life.

PAULINE   All right, I admit it would be nice to have some spare cash but ...

AMY   We could have gone on a decent holiday for once.

DEREK   We'll still be watching that goldfish bowl we call a telly.

PAULINE   I could have bought a new washing machine, and the fridge has almost had it.

DEREK   *(With great sadness)* This has definitely been the worst month of my entire life. All my efforts to secure our future prosperity have been washed down the drain. And if that wasn't enough, I'm responsible for giving away a picture that would have given us a lucrative payout.

AMY   *(Giving Derek a hug)* You weren't to know, Dad.

JOYCE   *(Entering from hall carrying some official documents)* Here we are. It's like winning the lottery.

DEREK   *(Glumly)* Is that supposed to be a joke?

JOYCE   I thought you'd be pleased, Derek. *(Pause)* You've always said you wanted to have a bit of cash.

DEREK   *(With disbelief)* You mean, you're going to share the money with us?

JOYCE   Of course I am. I wouldn't dream of keeping it all.

PAULINE   We don't want your money, Joyce.

DEREK   Shut up, darling. If Joyce wants to share her good fortune with us, who are we to argue?

PAULINE   *(To Derek)* You're nothing but a parasitic leech.

DEREK   *(To Joyce)* So what are you suggesting, a fifty, fifty split?

JOYCE   No, all I want is a hundred grand.

DEREK   *(With elation)* You mean we could be in line for four-hundred-thousand pounds?

JOYCE   Well, yes, it looks that way. All I've got to do is make one phone call to set the wheels in motion.

DEREK   *(Picks up the telephone receiver)* What's the number?

PAULINE   Just shut up, Derek.

DEREK   I only meant ... Um ... I thought Joyce's phone was out of action. *(Derek replaces receiver)*

JOYCE   I'll ring them the minute I get home.

PAULINE   *(Aside – to Joyce)* He doesn't deserve it, Joyce.

JOYCE   I know, but so what? If it makes him happy. We've only got one life. *(Pause)* In any case, the friend I'm moving in with is very well off. So I've no money worries now.

PAULINE   Thank you, so much.

DEREK   *(Kissing Joyce)* You're wonderful. *(Pause)* So where's the picture now?

JOYCE   I've left it round my house, for safe keeping.

PAULINE   Very wise.

JOYCE   I've just been talking to someone in our local supermarket about it, and he said you can't be too careful. He told me there's always art thieves on the lookout for easy pickings.

DEREK   And to think we had it on that very wall *(pointing to where picture had been)* for all those years.

AMY   This is fantastic. I've got myself a new boyfriend, and we've ...

PAULINE)
)   New boyfriend?
DEREK   )

AMY   Yes, Ben, my policeman friend.

DEREK   Oh well, at least he won't steal all our money. *(Pause)* This calls for a celebration. *(Goes to sideboard and gets out a bottle of champagne)*
This is turning out to be the best day of my life.

PAULINE   It's certainly had its ups and downs.

DEREK   *(Pouring out four glasses of champagne and handing them to everyone)* I'd like to propose a toast ...

REV. JONES   *(Entering from hall with Elizabeth)* I've got an announcement to make. *(Pause)* Elizabeth and I are moving in together.

PAULINE   But you've already done that.

REV. JONES   *(Smiling)* No, I mean, we're actually moving in together. *(Hugs Elizabeth)*

DEREK   Well done, Vicar. I think it's time for that toast. *(Getting another two glasses and filling them with champagne)*

PAULINE   Many congratulations. *(Hugging the Rev. Jones and Elizabeth)*

JOYCE   I'm so pleased for you both.

AMY   Best of luck.

DEREK   *(Handing champagne to Elizabeth and Rev. Jones)* To the good times. And may we all enjoy them.

```
PAULINE      )
JOYCE        )
AMY          )      The good times.
ELIZABETH    )
REV. JONES   )
```

(They all raise their glasses and drink. Amy wanders over to the window and looks out)

AMY   Joyce – did you leave your back door open?
JOYCE   No, I don't think so.
AMY   Well, there's two men outside getting into a car and one of them's holding something that looks like your picture.
JOYCE   Oh, no!
DEREK   It's those art thieves! *(Rushing to the door)* Come on everyone, let's see if we can stop them before they drive off.

(They all rush off through the hall exit)

BLACKOUT

13 Dec 2006

To Bob.,

Very many thanks for all your help with this play.

Ray Hopkins

LOVE AND MONEY

Farcical comedy ISBN 1852052686 4m 4f

A brand new farcical comedy from the master of the art who's previous plays have been a runaway success, being performed hundreds of times to full houses of delighted audiences. What happens when the family have a robbery and try to claim the insurance payment? Not a subject for a farcical comedy? Don't you believe it! The twist and turns, the intrigues, the misunderstandings and the falling-outs are as funny as ever. And all this takes place in one simple set

BY THE SAME AUTHOR

LOVE BEGINS AT FIFTY

This is the farce that started it all. First published in 1998, it was described by a critic as being up to the standards of the best of Ray Cooney - praise indeed! It has been performed all over the country with great success.

ISBN: - 185205 229 5 M3 F6

IT MUST BE LOVE

Another hilarious play by Ray Hopkins, with a frustrated wedding as the main topic. This farcical comedy has enjoyed a number of successful runs as a seaside summer show and packs them in at the local halls.

ISBN:- 185205 257 0 M6 F3

THE LOVE NEST

David and Janet Thompson were deeply in love when they married 32 years ago until Janet's mother moved in with them. A second honeymoon seemed a possible solution but it is doomed from the outset. Will true love triumph ? Only Tyson the mouse has the answer.

ISBN:-185205 258 9 M3 F7

SEND FOR OUR CATALOGUE to
HANBURY PLAYS

Keeper's Lodge, Broughton Green, Droitwich, Worcestershire WR9 7EE
or visit us on our website - www.hanburyplays.co.uk
Email - hanburyplays@onetel.com

IT MUST BE LOVE

A FARCICAL COMEDY IN TWO ACTS

by

RAYMOND HOPKINS

HANBURY PLAYS